Dominate Your Space

Dominate Your Space

Unleashing the Power of Your Product Managers

Greg DiCillo

Life Cycle Strategies, Inc.

To the Men and Women in Product Management who proudly embrace the role of "Product Champion" and the mission of adding value for your customer and your company.

Thanks…
My business partner and friend for 20 years, Ray Wymer, thank you for your calm and steady influence, unique perspectives, and for believing in the dream we call Life Cycle Strategies, Inc.

Kenn Ricci, my lifelong friend and mentor, thank you for your inspiration, guidance, and most of all your friendship.

J. J. a client and a friend, thank you for supporting the cause of product marketing and encouraging me to write this book.

Special Thanks…
My wife Tina, thank you for standing with me and believing in me.

TABLE OF CONTENTS

INTRODUCTION

The purpose of this book is not to tell you that your product managers aren't doing their jobs or that your organization is broken. If you're interested in modifying or reforming the way your product managers go about their business then you probably already have an idea that the results you are getting and the people you are hiring aren't meeting your expectations.

It's not uncommon for an organization to long for product managers who have the ability to think strategically and have a proactive vision and a market orientation to go with their ability to manage a business.

Unfortunately, what organizations often get are people who think in a more tactical way, who are reactive and product-centric and who are more prone to *project* management. And it isn't always easy to understand why the disparity exists between what an organization desires and what it gets from the product management side of its operation.

The purpose of this book is to help you identify where exactly that disparity is rooted in your organization and to help you establish a culture of high-performance product management that will benefit your *entire* organization.

Product management is a discipline; it's an ongoing way of thinking, and that means successful product managers need to be strategic in nature, embracing long-term, market-based thinking and planning. When they embrace these things, they drive an organization and fuel the development, marketing and sales efforts by managing and directing market-leading product portfolios.

Too often organizations are the ones to blame for the disparity between what they hope for from their product managers and what they get. Their structures and hierarchy force product managers to focus on *project* management and product *development* rather than on the larger, overall picture.

If you aren't getting the results you want from your product managers, your organization may have fallen into this trap. One thing we have seen, having trained and developed product managers in diverse industries such as electronics, computer communications, process controls and manufacturing, is that, in most cases, an organization's engineering resources and operations processes are well defined.

Conversely, in these same industries, most product management organizations' resources and processes are not clearly defined. As a result, new product managers—often recruited from operations and engineering—tend to revert back to a project or development perspective when promoted.

Because of their background and their training, these

product managers are internally focused people; they aren't market-driven. They are wired to think primarily from a design viewpoint and they tend to define the market from a product perspective. They think in terms of the technology they can bring to the product or what interesting features can be added rather than what the customers actually want or need. This type of thinking results in a *Field of Dreams* approach to product management that assumes that "if we build it, they will come."

More often than not, this mind-set is expensive and risky. While this occasionally works, product managers and their managers should recognize that a more sustainable approach to high-performance product management is to have product managers focused on their markets. By going into the field to uncover the real needs and requirements for new products and services, the product managers can create a product/market balance—a balance that is necessary to market leading product offerings.

Effective product managers base their recommendations around real market needs. They are outward-facing and bring the necessary information about customer needs into the organization. They represent the "voice of the customer" to the organization.

True product management and the managers who practice it need to be looked upon by an organization as a strategic element in the overall business strategy for growth. Good product managers are business owners unto themselves, focused on advancing the cause of their product line in conjunction with the goals of the larger organization. Their strategies must be aligned with corporate strategy and goals.

We will discuss the role of product manager in more detail

as we take you through the process of reshaping your organization, but for now it is important to know that what you are probably looking for in a product manager, and what we can deliver, is a return to some of the principles and mind-sets that were the very bedrock of your organization at its founding:

- The entrepreneurial spirit
- A product champion
- Market-focused

If, as an organization, you want more from your product management team, then you're probably asking very common questions in a quest to return to the attributes we've listed above: What's the best utilization of our resources? How can we be more market-focused? How do we get clarity at the front end of our product-development process?

What we've listed above are just some of the driving factors that can return your organization to what made it successful in the first place. But a word of warning here: this is not an easy process and is not for the faint of heart. Making a sea change at the organizational level takes real diligence and a commitment from the entire organization ***from the top down!***

Setting the foundation and getting the right agreements in place for appropriate planning takes dedication. This process is about creating market focus in your product managers and instituting a company-wide support system that embraces that mode of thinking and adds real structure and depth to it.

If you hope to keep your company on the cutting edge of product development, with a team that is proactive, you can't let your product managers focus inward. They must have a mandate to look beyond the borders of their own projects and product-development tasks into the realm of the needs and wants of their markets and customers.

Another key aspect we'll focus on in this book is that product management requires an ongoing process of analysis and decision-making. Product management requires constant attention and diligence to continually monitor changes in the markets that could affect the product portfolio and, ultimately, the organization's overall business plan.

Performing the role of product manager (heretofore referred to as "PM" when in the singular) requires a certain kind of individual, one that is not product-centric or merely tactical. It takes a person who understands that traditional business-to-business and industrial-product management, driven by sales and engineering, is no longer a viable way to create a sustainable competitive advantage. This inside-out approach needs to be supplanted by an outside-in model that leverages one's understanding of the markets, applications and customer usage to provide solutions that satisfy the needs and wants of the markets the product managers serve.

Market knowledge, with a focus on understanding the needs of the customers, is what allows companies to be leaders in their respective industries. Market-focused product managers foresee what customers might want or need and use this knowledge to devise solutions that customers want to buy. The challenge for business-to-business companies is to convert from a product-oriented organization to one that is market-centric. This book is designed to help you do just that.

CHAPTER 1

The Product Management Concept

The first step in any form of organizational improvement is a self-assessment. Of course a self-assessment is really just a way of establishing a baseline and, in the case of your organization, that baseline is a measure of how your company views product management, how your product managers are performing and what your organization is currently doing to support the product management function.

Before understanding how your organization stacks up, though, it's helpful to have a solid understanding of what we're referring to when we say "product management." While we've discussed this a bit already in the introduction, it may prove helpful to outline what we term "The Product Management Concept" before we move on to what product managers and their organizations ought to be doing.

The Product Management Concept really has two parts: (1) the attributes and outlooks of effective product managers and (2) the role they play in a larger organizational sense. As you can imagine, bringing these two elements together means having an organization-wide commitment to creating a culture that is conducive to high-performance product management.

Without the support of an organization that understands the benefits of a fully involved, market-focused product management team, product managers are left to their own devices and will default to whatever activities ensure their future employment. It's only human to do so, which means your organization must be committed to following through on any changes meant to upgrade the performance of your product managers.

Let's look at this concept in more depth.

The Product Management Concept

Product management is really about attitude and behavior more than just a list of responsibilities. These attitudes and behaviors cover three aspects of business, which we will discuss in detail after a brief synopsis of each:

1. **Organizational Aspect**: Enables focused and efficient management effort on products and markets.
2. **Management Aspect**: Allows the product manager the ability to manage the product line as a business.

3. **Strategic Aspect**: Focuses resources on strategic analysis of markets, segments, and emerging opportunities.

So what do each of these attributes look like in real life? Let's begin with the organizational aspect.

Organization

In a world where product managers are really "marketing" managers that focus their efforts on a given product, opportunities exist for them to recapture the entrepreneurial spirit that drove the creation of your organization in the first place. Because organizations become more conservative and bureaucratic as they expand, having this mind-set present within product management is an invaluable asset for staying ahead of the competition.

Most products are created because of a real or perceived gap in the marketplace. An entrepreneur sees that a potential customer has a problem and is looking for a solution. A decision is made to solve that problem with a product, and the marketplace moves forward.

That stance and attitude is really the way most entrepreneurs operate. They are marketers in that they are constantly looking at what the customer needs and wants. They ask themselves: "What can I do to capture the customer? What can I do to fill their needs or solve their problems so that my organization becomes the go-to supplier for what they need?"

In many ways, you want your product managers positioned as entrepreneurs in your organization with a focus on the product line and market segments. You don't want them focusing their attention on every little project or on every little detail of the product-development process. They are better utilized by having their eyes and ears focused on the market-place, constantly searching for opportunities and openings to position your organization in the minds of your customers and ahead of your competitors.

By allowing your product managers to operate in this capacity, you open the door for improvements in virtually every phase of your company's strategic planning—be it opera-tions, sales, marketing or even acquisitions. You enhance your strategic planning by enabling them to provide the facts and realities about their markets and the business to the planning process.

Next up and just as important is the management aspect of effective product management.

Management

What do we mean when we say that "a good PM will manage each product line or product offering as a separate business"?

Obviously a PM does not work apart from the larger organization. And, in fact, their goals and objectives must be aligned and driven by an up-to-the-minute understanding of where the organization is pointed in relation to the over-arching business plan. But as product managers they should look at their product lines as independent businesses within the company and as being in competition with other product lines in the markets they serve. To many organizations, viewing each product line as a separate business is a radical departure, especially when it comes to opening up financial data to the product managers.

Product managers need access to the financial data for their product lines in order to make better financial decisions and recommendations about their product mix. New product, product enhancements and extensions, and end-of-life strategies are incomplete if the basis of the recommendations made does not include the financial implications.

Managing the financials of the product line also enables product managers to assess product-pricing decisions by analyzing costs and profit margins. This allows them to recommend appropriate sales discounts, forecast operations to control inventory costs and focus engineering resources on appropriate product-line activities.

Effective product managers should be given the responsibilities and freedoms of independent business owners so that they view their mission as being just as critical as that of the entrepreneur. Without a clear mandate and support to attack the marketplace, many product managers fall into the trap of viewing their role as simply shepherding product-development activities in response to competitor products. Or, worse yet, to be merely implementers of strategies dictated by their superiors.

Strategic

That brings us to the strategic aspect of product management. You're probably thinking to yourself, "We all know that product managers should be forward-looking." But you also know that many of them aren't. So why not?

The reasons are many, and they include a lack of organizational support, a mentality that is more suited to the task at hand rather than one that may show up years down the road and even a fear of being wrong on any long-term prediction.

No one wants to be wrong, especially if they aren't rewarded for taking appropriate risks.

But product development can be a time-consuming process, which means the products that product managers are calling for need to be thought of well in advance of any timely release. Otherwise you'll find yourself continually reacting to your competitor's next technological breakthrough; you'll be left scrambling to come up with a response to your competitor's product offering, all the while wondering how you didn't see the opportunity first.

If your product managers are weighed down by thoughts of how each step in the development process is going to go, they'll see the individual trees and not the forest. Even the best product managers can be hamstrung by a lack of organizational commitment to strategic product management.

Innovative product managers see their product lines as opportunities to attack weaknesses or voids in the marketplace. They search out the demands of the consumers in the marketplace so that they have a solid footing for what will become critical in any high-performance product management culture: a forward-looking focus on planning that seeks to be proactive rather than reactive.

In our interactions with industrial manufacturing and service companies, we all too often find product managers who act only as firefighters rushing to catch up to a competitor's latest offering. They act this way because their organizations have focused them as such. With relative free reign and a mandate to analyze and attack the marketplace, effective product managers will become proactive planners and managers.

What Is the Role of the Product Manager?

First and foremost, the product manager's position is a marketing position. It cannot be confused with an engineering, product-development or *project*-management job. The PM is a marketer whose job it is to go out into the marketplace, interact with customers and then bring back recommendations to the organization based on those interactions. Product management's role is to balance the needs and requirements of their markets with the capabilities of the company while making sure that the product and market decisions align with corporate business objectives.

They are also tasked with analyzing competition in the marketplace, possible new market segments, the life cycle of each existing product under their purview and, just as important, with influencing the organization's leadership to act accordingly: in other words, a mix of hard analysis and soft skills.

So what role should a good PM play in the larger organizational picture? After all, even the best employees are at the mercy of the organizational structure to which they belong. And, what's further, management plays a large role in what product managers are allowed to do and what they are *mandated* to do.

Organizations are on a constant search for how best to use their resources. Times are tough and there isn't a lot of room to waste resources putting a solid employee on the wrong track in trying to help the company. So how can the PM best be used? What can these entrepreneurial, forward-thinking managers do to make your organization better?

There are a few things that, in our experience, have served organizations best in the use of effective product managers, and they compose a list of empowerment and responsibility. These include:

- ✔ Product managers have revenue and profit responsibility for their product offering.
- ✔ They define the market requirements an organization has in front of it.
- ✔ They match the product design and pricing to market needs.
- ✔ They recommend appropriate strategies.
- ✔ They manage the product portfolio throughout the life cycle.

We will delve further into how an organization can support their product managers in these responsibilities as we work through each of the subsequent chapters but it's important we focus for a brief moment on the last one on the list before moving along.

The words "life cycle management" will be used in this book to mean the ever-evolving plan that product managers must have as they focus on their markets. To be effective, they will have to be monitoring current product development, planning products for as many as three years down the road and gathering feedback from customers to inform future planning.

It is a cycle that aims to keep an organization moving forward based not on conjecture or what they want their expertise to be, but rather on what the market wants, how the market is responding to current products and what an organization can do to capture future market share based on that information.

So Why the Frustration?

If you've read the sections above and thought, "That's exactly what I want my product managers doing and who I want them to be," then you've probably also realized that you've known this for some time. You've also realized that you haven't found it yet, and, in our experience, you're not alone.

That's not because your organization hasn't been trying or that the right people aren't currently in your organization to get the job done. It may be that a few things are missing in the way that you recruit and develop talent and may also be that the right pieces aren't in place to create the culture of high-performance product management that you seek.

In our experience, though, the reason that organizations fail at finding and developing effective product managers has more to do with a few simple mistakes at the organizational level and also by the product managers already in place.

It's easy to make these mistakes, even with the best of intentions in mind, because keeping vigilance over the seemingly endless responsibilities associated with product management takes work and dedication. In the hectic world of faster time-to-market, shorter development cycles and increased competition, it is easy to lose focus.

Keeping an organization's pieces working toward one goal can be a monumental task. Product management and development are just two of the pieces in a much larger puzzle and, as such, they can easily be lost. We hope that this book helps you to find what it is you are missing in these aspects of your business so that the gaps can be filled and the resources you have can be used to their highest abilities.

In the next couple of chapters, we'll explore the specific

jobs of a product manager and the mistakes that product managers and their organizations most often make. We'll also look at what that means for the product management process in your organization.

In some ways, these mistakes are played out in slow motion for the entire organization to see because everyone is affected by reactionary product management. While these mistakes aren't exactly secrets, the solution to fixing them can sometimes be painstaking. So let's begin.

CHAPTER 2

What Exactly Does a Product Manager Do?

So what exactly does a product manager do? How many times have you or someone in your organization asked this question? Probably more than you'd like to admit. If you ask people in your organization to define the role of the PM, you will probably get as many definitions as the number of people you ask. While we defined the role in general in Chapter 1, the precise functions performed by effective product managers bears a deeper look.

The answer to what product managers do might have to do with a broader question: what do companies want from their product managers and what do they actually get? In the previous chapter, we talked about the attributes of effective product managers. So while all of the positive management attributes and job duties are universally desired by upper management when hiring product managers, the reality is that many times the marriage is an unhappy one. But why?

For now we'll focus on one aspect of the hiring process that comes up time and time again during our consulting and training engagements: the placement of seniority or familiarity over capability. It's a problem that isn't unique to the product management hiring process and is likely familiar to every human resources person tasked with filling a role.

It's not uncommon for organizations to assume that the people most intimately associated with a given product line would be the natural choice for the position of product manager. Most product managers are selected from other functional areas, most notably engineering, technical support and sales and customer service.

While these areas of expertise contribute to the role, they are not nearly enough. People pulled from these roles tend to lack other critical dimensions required for the role, including the capability to influence other functions in the organization, proficiency in their understanding of the markets and competency as business managers and leaders.

This is not to say that in all cases these individuals cannot be product managers. It is quite possible that some may have the skills or aptitudes required to fulfill the role; however, if, when hiring product managers, all the aspects of the role are not considered, you are more likely to end up with tactical, internally focused individuals rather than the proactive strategic business managers you expect.

We'll deal more with the mistakes organizations make in subsequent chapters, but for now let's look at what product managers should be doing—what organizations really want from their product managers but aren't getting.

These are the five basic areas in which a PM has to be capable: as an owner, marketer, strategist, planner and manager.

Owner: The product manager, in the role as "owner," manages the revenue and profitability of the offering.

While product lines are not literally individual businesses, the maneuverings required to keep a product line relevant are similar in nature to what the overall organization has to do to stay alive. Addressing product-line issues and strategy only at the corporate level dilutes the view of the markets they serve and the effects of the unique competitors they may encounter.

PMs must cater their strategies toward making the product line sustain itself in terms of revenues and profits, just as the CEO of the larger body does. What's the point of creating a product line that doesn't make money for the larger organization?

This responsibility is a must for the PM because it keeps their focus aligned with the ultimate goal of product management: contributing to the overall financial health of the company. The ownership role must be made very real to a product manager. It cannot be a pep talk or a slogan. When organizations don't provide product managers access to their costs and don't hold them accountable for revenue and profit, they effectively negate key components of the business-owner role, and the business-owner role is one of the components that feeds into the entrepreneurial spirit.

We call this existence being an "intrapreneur," which is a different way of saying that product managers hold virtually none of the ultimate authority enjoyed by entrepreneurs and yet, to be successful, they must think as though they do.

Marketer: The product manager defines the market requirements.

PMs should frequently ask themselves a few questions: How well do I understand the customers and the segments, and are there others I can explore? How well am I getting out into the marketplace? How well is my product positioned against my competitor's? In what stage of the life cycle are my products? What are the dynamics in my markets and how are they changing?

These questions are really the embodiment of the strategic mind-set a PM must have. Dedicating hundreds of thousands of dollars and thousands of man-hours to the research and creation of a new product or service is a decision that haunts many organizations. Large industrial organizations are like the super-tankers of the business world; they do not stop or turn quickly. As a consequence, leadership in these organizations is sometimes conservative to a fault. With an informed product management organization, these decisions are made with a fuller understanding of the long-term implications.

When you ask the question: "Where do I take market risks and is a new opportunity really worth the investment?" a good PM should step in and help your organization understand the opportunities in the marketplace by giving them context. That means understanding what each opportunity could mean for both the product line and organization in real dollars and cents, and being able to look down the road and predict how different scenarios and decisions might play out.

Planner: The product manager matches product and pricing to the market needs.

A good PM relates the opportunity to the product and asks, "How well do we understand the priorities and the needs of our customers? What is the market window for the product and can we dominate the market space? What is the opportunity to gain market share? Do we have the resources and competency to win? Is it sustainable?"

A PM may at any given time have a laundry list of projects that need to be done, but they must be prioritized. Industrial product development can be a lengthy process. Product managers need to be thinking as a planner would think: long-term. They can't just add new information to the to-do list without any basis for the order and priority in which things ought to be done.

As planners, they understand that the resources and time of their organization are limited and seek to understand what the organization should be doing and why. They also recognize that planning means making trade-offs based on the best market information and then effectively executing the plan. At the same time, effective planning can be ruined if an organization fails to follow through on a product manager's recommendations.

Opportunities must be tethered to existing product lines or future product lines that are realistic for the organization. It's one thing to understand where an opportunity exists; it's quite another to know how to best take advantage of it. If there is a market opportunity for electric motors or industrial controls then what should it look like? Which price range best suits the organization's capabilities?

These are not easy questions, and a PM needs to be on top of the market to understand the answers. Fitting a square peg in a round hole is not going to work in the harsh realm of the open market. If a PM looks at an opportunity and realizes that the organization is not positioned to take advantage of it, they must make that known.

And, conversely, if they feel that one of their products is right for a market segment, they should say, "Here is the price range we should be looking at and here are the features that are worth creating for our product."

Your product managers are of course not the only ones in the organization that ought to be planning long-term. There is a hierarchy to planning in any effective organization, with product-line plans feeding up into portfolio plans, which ultimately should mate with the corporate strategic plan and business objectives of the entire organization. Unfortunately, we run into too many product managers who are not informed of organizational goals and are given little context in which to create their strategic plans.

Strategist: The product manager recommends strategies based on a thorough analysis of the market.

Product managers don't have power over the organization they work for. It's a dilemma we'll discuss in the next section, but suffice it to say that a PM needs to be good in the art of persuasion.

Like a good chess player, a PM needs to understand timing and the impact of certain moves. They ask themselves, "How well do I leverage my understanding of the market? How do I bring my product into the market at the right time against the competition so that I can differentiate it from others?"

Because timing is such an integral part of a product's

success in the marketplace, real strategists are able to organize their moves ahead of a launch in such a way as to beat the competition. Oftentimes first is best, but not always. If delaying a launch is the best thing for your organization, how will you know? Your product managers will tell you.

Strategic thinking at the product management level is critical. Most companies consider strategy to be something that is done only at the executive level and, in most cases, it is. However, there is a need for product managers to be involved in the strategic process because corporate strategy informs product decisions, and product and market information compiled by product managers can inform corporate strategic thinking.

Recognizing the synergy between corporate strategic planning and multi-generational product planning gives a tremendous boost to the development of the strategic plan and, more importantly, goes a long way to aligning product portfolio strategies with the corporate strategy.

At the product-line or portfolio level, strategic planning forces the product managers to think about product life cycles from innovation and new development to end-of-life and rationalization. This longer-term view provides a broader scope and requires product managers to look out and plan for growth rather than simply focusing on short-term and internal activities.

As strategists, the product managers will outline a broader vision for their product portfolio and be better suited to provide road maps that take all aspects of the product life cycle into account.

Manager: The product manager manages the product portfolio throughout the life cycle.

Launching a product is not the end of the process for a product manager. If a product line is to survive (or be eliminated, if necessary), it must be with the informed feedback of the marketplace. That same feedback informs the planning and strategy of the PM and ultimately any redesign of the product or its replacement.

It is an ongoing process that must be managed in its entirety. The role of PM is an active one; it requires constant vigilance and the know-how to understand how products are moving in the marketplace and how the dynamics of the marketplace are evolving. Markets never stand still.

So much of what an organization does, whether it be operations, marketing or sales, is based on the future plans for a product. Resources are constantly wasted on products that have no future in the marketplace because product managers are not monitoring the life cycle. It is much easier to focus on new products that excite the company leadership than it is to manage existing lines. Yet existing product lines, as mundane as they appear, are a key to a company's ability to drive growth and fuel investment in new or emerging market segments.

Furthermore, product managers without a full picture of the way a product relates to their customers' needs will waste time and energy installing design features in a product because one customer has requested it. But is it worth the time and money? Is this customer representative of the entire marketplace and do they provide enough business to justify the costs?

If your organization is multi-line or multi-brand, you know that an effective product mix or portfolio can help avoid leeching and stagnation. With an eye toward the marketplace, a real manager will hopefully be able to understand the movements that affect that mix.

As you can see, the competencies required of a PM are

complex. So after examining what it is they *should* be doing, it might help to identify some of the things that a PM should *not* be doing. We've seen time and again that organizations, because of limited resources or outmoded tradition, ask their product managers to get involved in all kinds of things that are not conducive to being a PM in its most productive sense.

A good first step toward a more effective PM is to **avoid** having your product managers too involved in these three areas:

- **Project Management**: Managing a product line does not mean that every subset of tasks needed to accomplish a product manager's goals should draw their attention. Projects are secondary when compared to the long-term thinking required by a PM who strives to put their product line at the forefront in the market. PMs must manage the process but not the projects because they are responsible for overseeing the broader vision relating to time-to-market and alignment of products to markets. The projects and the deliverables should be managed at the functional organizations by those responsible for the actual deliverable.

- **Marketing Communications**: While being a PM is a marketing job in nature, it is only such because it focuses on markets. That does not mean that product managers are responsible for ad campaigns designed at moving inventory. While the PM is responsible for providing the strategy, points of differentiation, target markets and value proposition, marketing communications, including generating ads and printing materials, should be left to the marketing department or agency to execute at the direction of the product manager.

- **Product Development**: When it comes to making a product right for the consumers, there are many hands and disciplines involved. That means someone needs to guide the overall process of making the product offering work for the consumer and also to update it when necessary. These tasks fall to a product developer, not a product manager. A product manager's focus is on the requirements of the market for the product. He or she needs to inform the product developers of trends in the marketplace so that the product can be updated, but the product managers are not responsible for making the necessary changes.

These activities are engaged in by product managers as a result of their own misguided efforts and sometimes because of organizational problems. In the next couple of chapters, we'll discuss the common mistakes that product managers make in their roles, but we'll also talk about what organizations sometimes do to ruin the partnership as well.

CHAPTER 3

The Product Manager's Dilemma

If, after reading the previous descriptions of effective product managers, you're asking, "How can my product managers be owners, planners, marketers, strategists and leaders when they don't actually control the resources at their disposal?" then you've just uncovered one of the most defining aspects of product management and why it is so tricky: **The Product Manager's Dilemma**.

The Product Manager's Dilemma is the realization that product managers have responsibility and accountability for the success of the product line but have little or no authority over the resources that are ultimately needed to be successful. It is *the* reason the soft skills of product management outweigh any and all technical or product expertise.

Product managers are not CEOs in a literal sense, even though we encourage organizations to treat them as entrepreneurs and business leaders. That means they don't have the authority to force decisions that are favorably biased towards their view of the marketplace.

So the PM has power in a limited sense, but does not have the authority to move the resources of the larger organization. Despite being in charge of the product line, these managers rarely have the final say or immediate authority to make wholesale changes and so they must be capable of making recommendations and confident enough to defend them. That means product managers must be credible, and credibility comes from self-confidence, knowledge, preparedness and the ability to effectively influence decisions and communicate strategy.

Unfortunately, we rarely see these attributes from product managers. As a result, even product managers that are in charge of hundred-million-dollar product lines are sometimes incapable or fearful of making recommendations with any conviction.

Much of the credibility a PM has or does not have is based in the substance of their recommendations. To achieve the level of credibility that a product manager needs to effectively manage their product lines, they must communicate and procure the resources they require to be successful. They have to overcome the product manager's dilemma. The key to overcoming the dilemma is to develop five influencing techniques:

1. Product/Market Expertise—The best way for a PM to establish credibility is to become the expert in their markets. The real value a PM

brings to an organization is the understanding of the needs and wants of the markets. The true measure of credibility comes when people within the organization come to the PM for their advice.

2. Leadership—Product managers are champions of the product line and, as such, must always be out front. As leaders, they must direct the resources that are at their disposal and be accountable for the outcomes. Credibility comes from standing up for what they believe to be true and the courage of their convictions when making decisions and recommendations.

3. Idea Generation—Product managers must be capable of generating ideas. Going into meetings with a blank sheet of paper just doesn't help a product manager's credibility. If they are truly experts in their fields, they will know the needs of the markets they serve and have ideas for how to best position their products.

4. Relationship-Building—An effective PM knows how to build bridges between himself and the other functional areas in order to get things done. The PM needs everyone in the organization to perform if he expects to succeed.

5. Planning—Credible product managers work with short-term and long-term plans as their guides. This allows them to effectively navigate through the constant bombardment of

ideas, requests and issues that they deal with each day. It allows them to make decisions and recommendations in a more timely fashion and with more confidence. You would not believe how few product managers have long-term plans.

Product managers who hone these techniques will be much more likely to overcome the dilemma between their responsibilities and their lack of authority. Simply honing these skills doesn't resolve the dilemma, though. Organizational changes that define the rules of engagement, allied with appropriate interfaces, must also be created to allow the flow of information and accountability required to be successful. We will elaborate more on this in the next couple of chapters.

CHAPTER 4

The Thirteen Most Common Product Manager Mistakes

Now that we know what product managers are *supposed* to be doing, it's informative to look at what many of them *are* doing. If an organization's product managers are not providing the results an organization desires from the position, the root cause could be any number of things. In our experience, there are trends in the mistakes that product managers make. We've found that thirteen common mistakes appear repeatedly in organizations where the product managers are failing to deliver.

While these mistakes are listed here individually, they are often connected to one another in a manager incapable of handling the position. It's never easy to criticize or replace a long-time employee, but the reality is that some people are not meant for the job.

Alternately, it is very likely that the product managers you have are making these mistakes because of unclear goals, a reward system that steers them away from strategic thinking or even a lack of support from their counterparts in the rest of the organization. Many times product managers turn out to be effective once these organizational problems are remedied.

Regardless of the mistakes your product managers make, they cannot be separated from any organizational flaws that may exist. We will discuss those flaws in the next chapter, but for now we want you to understand that grading a product manager's performance in the context of a flawed organizational support system is premature.

The thirteen most common mistakes product managers make include:

1. *Working without a Written Plan*

Related to strategic market planning, and what you could call the fruit of that labor, is the written plan. In our experience, we have run into a lot of product managers who don't have written plans for their product lines. In fact, only 30 percent of product managers we've encountered have a written product line or portfolio plan!

In some cases the company does not require written plans so the product managers get away with seat-of-the-pants management. In some cases, the company itself doesn't have a corporate strategic plan in writing, which is an even bigger problem.

Planning is a discipline and in many organizations there's not an appetite for it. Annual budgeting becomes a surrogate for a strategic plan. Product plans are not required and, worse, aren't used if they do exist. It should, in fact, be the opposite. Product managers should be saying, "This is where we're headed and so these are the resources we'll need. Here are the product requirements and here is the written business justification for each."

Product managers should have a written plan because it crystallizes the product requirements and it helps to guide the resources of the organization. The written plan becomes the compass that a PM uses to navigate on a day-to-day and month-to-month basis.

The lack of a written plan can lead to wild changes in strategy because no one can point to specific reasons for why things are being done. That instability is toxic to effective product development. Written plans provide the documentation, reasoning and commitments to drive what is being done. They also provide the focus for changes and modifications, which, when documented, add clarity and keep all of the resources focused and on track.

2. Lack Strategic Marketing Skills

Many product managers talk about doing market analysis, but most don't ever get close enough to their customers or prospects to fully understand the market for their products. They don't learn about customers' needs, wants or unmet needs, how they can differentiate their product in the marketplace or which adjacent markets might be explored to help drive sales.

Market analysis has been relegated to a once-per-year event for many product managers when, in fact, market analysis needs to be an ongoing process rather than an event—a constant in any effective product manager's activities.

Strategic market analysis is needed in several important ways. First, a PM must know the unmet needs, trends and buying motivations of their customers. They must understand how their markets are segmented and the diverse needs that exist between them. Secondly, they must know and understand the branding, strengths, weaknesses, strategies and vulnerabilities of their competitors. And finally a PM must turn the microscope on to their own product line and do an in-depth analysis of their own brand's heritage, its image and its strengths and weaknesses.

Markets are not static, even in industrial applications where lead-time for a given product can be months or even years. In fact, in these applications, strategic market analysis is even more important because of the length of the research and development that goes into large and complex products.

The level of commitment to strategic market planning a PM has—and how effective she is at it—makes a significant difference in her product planning and 4P strategies. Product managers who market strategically will be better aware of their organization's strengths, have products better positioned in their markets and will target their market segments better. As a result, they will ultimately develop better product requirements that align with customer needs, which can ultimately lead to a dominant market position.

3. *No Life Cycle Plan*

Life cycle planning is the centerpiece of the product manager's role. Product managers must know when to develop new products, when to rationalize old products and how to effectively manage existing products. Managing a product portfolio is like managing a mutual fund in that a PM needs to be capable of optimizing the product portfolio by knowing when to get rid of underperformers, how to leverage good performers and when to introduce new products that enrich the portfolio over time.

There is an evolution to every portfolio and product managers need to keep a mix of offerings and strategies at hand, including end-of-life strategies. In our experience, there is such an emphasis on new product development in many organizations that life cycle planning goes unattended.

Without a close monitoring of existing products, an organization is wasting market potential for each one, allowing sales or new opportunities to be lost in the rush for the latest and greatest product. It is the product manager's responsibility to make sure someone is keeping an eye on the ball. This means that every new product-development opportunity must be contemplated within the context of life cycle planning.

It's not uncommon to see product managers introduce new products to the market while never asking what the launch means for their existing product portfolio. They have to be asking how a new product development impacts existing products and markets. What product line holes are being filled, what product overlaps are being created?

Product managers are responsible for asking themselves the questions no one else is capable of answering. If they have a true grasp of the marketplace, they should be able to determine the direction of the product line, the focus of product developments and the rationalization activities that must take place to optimize product-line performance.

It is never a good sign when your product managers say,

"I've got so many products in my product line I can't manage them." This is indicative of someone who is not life cycle planning.

4. *Manage Without Financial Metrics*

Many of our clients say that their product managers are responsible for the financials of their product lines, which is something we encourage. The problem is that these same companies often don't provide their product managers with access to all of the costs of products or the development costs for new products. Given that, how can product managers know if their product lines are profitable?

The two most common responses we hear are, "Product managers can set the market price but sales controls pricing and discounting," or, "Product managers can't manage to a profitability goal because they don't manage all of the resources."

If you are going to ask your product managers to manage their product lines as a business owner might, then you must give them the ability to see top-line and bottom-line numbers. The PM needs to be able to answer the question, "What is the product line bringing to the table from a profit standpoint?"

Sometimes the only costs a PM can monitor are the development costs. But as business owners, they need to be asking, "How is the product line's profitability? Are we selling or discounting the products too much? Are we effectively forecasting and managing inventory?"

A PM can't be expected to hit his gross margin targets when he doesn't know his costs. He can't effectively understand how the product is positioned in the segments if he doesn't have visibility into the pricing and discounting pressures in his channels. He can't effectively assess operational issues if they don't have a feel for supply-and-demand changes in their segments and he can't effectively assist operations with inventory and cost containment if he doesn't have access to critical financial information.

It is not necessary for managers to do the jobs of these functional areas, but with appropriate financial data the PM can analyze the product line and make decisions and recommendations relative to his product portfolio that can be beneficial to the other functional areas.

If a PM is being held responsible for the financials of her product line, she must push for greater access to the relevant numbers.

5. Fail to Lead

The product manager role is a leadership role. Not all product managers realize this and just as many organizations suffer the same misunderstanding. Leadership is a quality that is hard to define, but it's perhaps most obvious in its absence and without it an organization is usually late to market and playing catch-up.

It would be easy to assume that this is a problem inherent to only smaller organizations, the assumption being that, in larger organizations, product managers who have climbed the ladder exhibited a high level of leadership ability already. Not true.

Many product managers, even those in charge of hundred-million-dollar product lines, don't take the mantle of leadership. They don't try to be the center-point of the discussion about which products ought to be developed or eliminated or updated. They allow themselves to be dragged around by other people who are more assertive and as a consequence the entire organization may be hurt.

This is symptomatic of a larger problem in the corporate structure, whereby the squeaky wheel gets the grease. Whoever is assertive enough to take charge over a discussion receives priority in determining what happens. Without clearly defined roles, this condition goes unchecked.

If product managers know their markets as well as they ought to, then they should be considered the leading authorities on them. Leadership, though, means taking risks and making trade-offs. It means opening yourself up to criticism when a product fails or when your judgment is wrong. That's a burden most people don't want and so they allow others to take charge. They do what other people tell them to do. But it's *their* product line.

Product managers need to know their business and they need to make recommendations about the product line that are based in the realities of their business. Being able to stand up and say, "As the leader of the product line, I feel this is the direction we need to go" is an ability many product managers long for but fear. So most end up saying, usually implicitly, "I'll give you my opinion but wait for you to make the decisions."

Product managers need to exhibit leadership and move things forward. If a PM knows their business, they should feel confident enough to speak up and say so. There are three types of managers: those that make things happen, those that watch things happen and those that wonder what happened. The expectations most organizations have for their product managers are that they will make things happen. If they aren't, then this may be the problem.

6. *Myopic Product Focus*

Product managers who exhibit myopic product focus are those who fail to define the "whole product," and see only the features and functionality of the physical product. This is a mistake since intangible aspects of the product, such as warranty, support, service, installation, etc., are all part of the customer's decision-making process. Focusing on features without looking at the whole product minimizes your product's overall value in the form of lost opportunities.

Product requirements must include an understanding of all of the needs that are driving customer decisions. A PM should strive to understand the broader picture of what the customer is trying to accomplish and what problems they are trying to solve. A full understanding of these things helps to inform the product solution rather than simply defining product features.

When the broader picture is understood, product managers can actually start to develop product solutions that include the tangible and intangible qualities that customers are looking for. This is where product managers can bring added value to the customers that create sustainable competitive advantage. This is especially important for companies with mature products or that are competing in mature and evolving markets.

7. *Following a Single P Strategy*

The one thing product managers have control over is the marketing mix, the ability to create product strategies that utilize the 4Ps: product, price, place and promotion. Unfortunately, many product managers don't recognize or don't understand the necessity of employing all four Ps as part of their product-line strategies. Instead, they tend to focus on only one or two.

If a PM is too technical in his thinking, he may see only product solutions when problems arise. If the product isn't selling, he'll say, "We'll fix it with the product; we'll make the product better." The product is not always the weakness and it's not always the solution.

Place, promotion or pricing can be a problem. Maybe the product is in the wrong channel or the sales team has missed the mark in establishing the value proposition. Maybe the product is poorly priced for the target markets. Maybe the products are not appropriately targeted to the market segments.

Product managers can't be single-P focused because it can lead to expenditures in product development that are unnecessary or misguided. If a proper analysis of the market has been done during product development, the product should be meeting the needs of the customers. Even good products can be affected by a poorly planned marketing campaign or pricing strategy, so any good PM should look at the "easy" fixes first: can we change the price or simply do a better job of explaining the product's value to our potential customers?

While altering the product may be an appropriate product decision, product managers should make sure they have assessed all four Ps as part of their product-line strategy before going through with an alteration.

8.   *Driven by a Single Customer*

In the business-to-business arena, companies usually have one or two very large customers who heavily influence product decisions. While that may work when dealing with just a few customers, a PM dealing in the larger market(s) has to be mindful that the products and features requested by one customer are not always what others in the market are looking for.

Any decision to modify or keep a given product needs to be made based on the market for the product rather than the desires of a single customer. It can be tempting to bow to a large customer because they represent a good bit of the business. But before spending time and money on a development, take a look at the numbers and what might come of denying the customer their request.

We're not suggesting that product managers ignore specific customer wants. On the contrary, the PM, when assessing a large customer request, must be capable of determining whether the request is viable for commercialization or is special enough that it should be made available only as a customer special. Many times, getting this wrong results in "special" products being commercialized for the broader market only to find that these specialized products do not sell commercially.

If you are struggling with an overload of part numbers with limited sales volume, you may want to ask yourself whether these products were really nothing more than one-off special requests for a single customer rather than a solution to the broader market. If your product managers aren't focused on the market as a whole, the consequence of a product proliferation will be more negative than positive.

9. Following the Competition

Following the leader means product management by the competition. When a PM isn't comfortable in the market, he simply reacts to what competitors are doing. There are many problems with this, but the most obvious is that a product manager's competitors might be way off the mark in their market predictions. Following them might be the fastest way to failure.

In the "Fail to Lead" section, we spoke about the risk that leadership entails and how many product managers seek to avoid that risk by deferring decision-making to a colleague or subordinate. The same thing happens on a larger scale when a PM relinquishes planning to his competitors.

Unfortunately, this kind of "leadership" is all too common. Afraid to risk making a public mistake or of being stuck in the weeds, many product managers either wait to hear what a competitor has in the works or, worse yet, wait until their competitor releases a product to the market.

The product managers who follow their competitors are assuming that the competitors know what they are doing. Ask yourself this question: "If these mistakes are common among all product managers, why would we believe that the competitors have a better feel for the market than we do?"

The problem of course is that even if the competition is on the right track for their market space, this does not guarantee that releasing a particular product type is the right decision for your company.

By hitching his organization's wagon to a competitor, the PM takes on even more risk than he might face in simply analyzing the markets and tailoring a product to his own company.

10. Rely on Gut Feeling Over Facts

While it's easy to admire someone with a strong intuition and feeling for the market, the fact remains that without hard data to support decisions, a PM is in the dark. How can they know that their decisions aren't completely off-base? How much better off would they be with research to support a given position?

What's more, influencing decision-makers is made more difficult when the decision-maker doesn't share the same gut feeling. Of course, some level of trust has to be present between a PM and his management, but trust isn't enough. Allocating tens of millions of dollars is not done lightly and in some ways product managers have to build cases for their ideas.

Effectively managing this balance is really a battle waged by the PM with himself. How much does he rely on his knowledge of the marketplace versus just raw data? The scale is tipped toward fact-based reckoning when he realizes that knowing something about the market and convincing others of it are two different games.

Ultimately it is up to the PM to convince his management of the validity of his proposals. He has to get them to accept his judgment as valid, even if his decisions carry with them some risk.

Risk is inherent in any business decisions, but it can be made more palatable if built on a pairing of research and intuition. With an experienced, fact-based, proven leader in the product manager's role, management is more likely to offer its trust.

11. Managing When They Should Influence

We've spoken about the product manager's dilemma: that they have little authority and a great deal of responsibility. As a consequence, many product managers make the mistake of focusing their efforts on managing the resources over which they have no control rather than managing the processes and influencing the resources they can affect.

One key to the product management process is working in a cross-functional matrix by using the product plan as the compass for affecting the product manager's sphere of influence. A cross-functional matrix is the structure that describes any business that requires cooperation from multiple camps for project completion. Understanding how to operate in this paradigm allows for directing the resources allocated by virtue of the plan document. The mistake many product managers make is that once the resources are applied to given projects, they fail to keep these resources on track or to hold management accountable for promises made in regard to these resources.

An effective PM will use the plan and the associated agreements resulting from the plan to hold others accountable. They can then use influence to keep resources focused on the common goal. When product managers try to manage the personnel without utilizing the plan, they risk making the project a personal agenda rather than a conscious business decision. Plans help to make things official.

12. Major in Minor Things

Adopting a focus on minutiae comes from having a tactical background and is a symptom of discomfort in leading. Instead of delegating to other parts of an organization, product managers try to handle all things relating to their product line.

Product managers waste valuable time attempting to solve problems that others in the organization may be better suited to handling. Examples of this include: dealing with technical support issues rather than relying on sales and technical support to handle them and diving into engineering issues and taking it upon themselves to resolve the problem personally.

Obviously if there are major issues with a major client, the PM could stay close to the problem as it is being addressed, but a product manager's job is not customer service, nor is it engineering.

Trying to do all things creates a domino effect; if a PM shows willingness to over-extend himself once, others in the organization will start expecting it. The consequence is that a PM will be called upon to handle more and more of the activities that are clearly the responsibility of others in the organization.

13. Work Only Within Their Comfort Zone

We have found that product managers have a tendency to migrate toward doing the things they like or are comfortable doing. And since most product managers come into the position from another field (product development, sales, etc.), they focus on those areas to the exclusion of all others.

Some aspects of the product management role involve capabilities learned from these previous positions, which is good, but these skills are not the only ones required to manage the product portfolio. Discomfort with market-segment analysis, financial analysis, planning and strategy should not preclude a PM from working outside of her comfort zone.

The greatest value a PM can bring to her organization is developing the broader skill sets that lead to a better understanding of her markets. That means more effective development of strategies, and increased understanding of the financials surrounding the product line, especially those that drive business growth.

Product managers that work only in their comfort zones limit their own ability to grow in the role but, more importantly, limit the growth potential for their product line and ultimately the ability for the company to achieve its growth objectives.

The important thing is that product managers and their managers recognize these mistakes and take the appropriate action to fix or avoid them. Modifying the behavior of your product managers starts by understanding what they are doing and why. If you want high-performance product management, you have to create the environment that is conducive for it and that starts with the elimination of these common mistakes.

While it's clear from this chapter that product managers are capable of many mistakes, it should be clear that product managers rarely make mistakes in a vacuum. In a number of cases, PM mistakes are caused by organizational mistakes. We'll discuss these in the next chapter.

CHAPTER 5

The Eight Most Common Organizational Mistakes

While we've shown in Chapter 4 that product managers do indeed make mistakes, they are but one part of a larger picture. In this chapter we'll discuss some of the more common mistakes organizations make in handling their product managers. Because most companies desire strategic and forward-looking business leadership from their product managers, it's crucial that they actively support the behaviors they want to see.

A clear, well-understood definition and structure is crucial to effective product management because product managers depend so highly on those around them. With this structure in place, and the mistakes listed in this chapter eliminated, a true set of measures can be established and monitored.

The eight most common organizational mistakes include:

1. *Corporate Culture That Lacks Sound Strategic Planning Processes*

Is your organization one that believes in and has a discipline for planning, not just budgetary planning, but also market and business and industry planning? If not, then there is a disconnect between what you want in a PM and what is being practiced by the organization.

As we've said before, product management revolves around planning and strategy. If that planning doesn't happen at the corporate level, the company as a whole is more reactionary. It responds to the latest whims of the marketplace and then dictates down to product management what should be done, negating any predictive analysis a product manage might have done.

Companies that plan long-term strategies and have a vision for where the company is going can align product plans to meet these corporate strategies. It's important for the executive leadership of an organization to ask themselves if product management is aligned with corporate strategy. Is the overall strategic plan getting communicated, especially to the product managers? And is that communication going the other way? Are the product managers feeding information up to corporate leadership that will help with strategic planning for the future?

It's not unusual for us to hear product managers say, "What is the corporate strategy?" or, "We've never heard the strategy." This lack of planning impacts product management success.

2. Fail to Define PM Roles and Responsibilities

We see this problem time and again, and it has two parts: failing to clearly define the roles of product managers for the sake of the product managers and failure to define these roles and responsibilities to the rest of the organization.

Product managers must have clearly defined roles, not just a list of tactical activities that they are required to perform. This is especially important because if their roles are not clearly defined, it makes it difficult for them to work effectively with the critical resources they require.

Without company-defined roles, each individual in the organization defines the product manager's responsibilities based on what they perceive the role to be. If you are wondering if this problem exists in your company, just go around and ask the people that interface most closely with the product managers to define the role. It should take only a few queries to get your answer.

The bottom line is this: when the people in an organization aren't sure what the product managers' roles are, random responsibilities get thrust upon the product managers because, after all, "it's their product." Conversely, when product managers are unsure of what their role is, any definition, regardless of the source, will do.

3. Lack Clearly Defined Rules of Engagement Between Product Management and Functions

What is it that is expected from the other parts of an organization as they relate to product management? The answer to that question should be well-defined organization-wide. Just as it is important to clarify the role and job description of the PM, it is also important to clearly define how the organization will interface with product management.

This includes outlining exactly which role each functional area plays in product success and what expectations the functional areas and product managers should have of one another. The fact is that all aspects of the organization have a hand in product success. While most will say they understand this concept, many simply aren't living up to it.

For product managers to be successful leading cross-functional teams, the organization must set the guidelines and responsibilities for these interactions and be willing to enforce their guidelines to ensure that all parties work together toward product success.

There is a give and take in this process and the functional areas need to assess the requirements laid out by the product manager and report back on what they can realistically contribute. When rules of engagement aren't clearly defined, the PM gets all the responsibility and, in some cases, the functional areas abdicate responsibility or don't do anything at all. The consequence is finger-pointing, and that costs time and money due to delays.

4. *Hiring the Wrong People*

We've seen many times that individuals are hired for the PM role without an explanation of what their employer really wants. Worse yet, the wrong person is hired for the job. If you're a product-driven company and you hire someone from product development, you'll probably find someone that lacks the market, industry, sales and channel knowledge you're hoping for. Most people are hired from product development for their product knowledge, but these other areas of knowledge are not as easily developed.

As a result of poor selection, the people who are placed in the roles are good specialists but not good generalists. They may not be able to plan or perform business management and strategy development, and those skills are important to product management success.

Organizations tend to hire people for the role who are tactically oriented because, on the surface, someone from engineering or sales might seem promising; they may understand customers or have a deep understanding of the product. The real question, though, is whether they are geared toward fixing problems instead of planning long-term.

Sometimes organizations hire people because they want someone to simply monitor their products. This may be okay for a mature product line but it is devastating for a product line with high growth potential. And there is another consequence: credibility. Once a product manager's credibility is lost, their ability to influence is lost. This has a trickle-down effect and impacts their success.

Many of the people we see in the PM role are hard workers. But that isn't enough. They are doers, not leaders, and you must find leaders to fill these positions. By making short-sighted hiring decisions like the ones we've listed, you miss the opportunity to build a solid organization centered on skills, knowledge and ability.

5. *Failing to Leverage Product Managers in Strategic Marketing*

Many industrial and business-to-business companies look at product managers as extensions of product development or as sales support. But strategic marketing means understanding enough of the functionality of the product to position it in the marketplace against fierce competition. It's more than short-term sales or product features.

Product managers utilized in a strategic marketing role add value to an organization by filling a void that many companies are missing. They fill this void by knowing the uses and applications of their products, effectively targeting markets, differentiating products within portfolios as well as between competitive products and then identifying new and emerging markets.

If an organization turns this position into a strict sales support or product-development function, then they also miss out on key marketing communications. Product managers that are allowed to perform strategic marketing can answer questions like, "What are the value propositions for the product in each segment?" and "How are we going to position ourselves against our competitors?"

When the PM is viewed as an extension of development, the organization misses out on leveraging the marketing mix when targeting products in each segment, and that's a big miss.

6. *Lack Appropriate Metrics to Measure and Modify Behavior*

Businesses all say they want visionary business leaders in the product management position. But when we review the job descriptions some organizations have, the opposite appears true.

Too many companies have very tactical metrics, such as how many products the PM can create in a year or how fast products are pushed through the pipeline. These metrics don't measure how effective a product manager's planning, vision and long-term directions are.

Some job descriptions we've seen even have internally focused goals like catalogue updates and price books. What these job descriptions do is tell the product manager that his job depends on tactical work. Product managers are extremely motivated individuals who will do whatever they need to do to get ahead, sometimes at the expense of what really needs to be accomplished. They see targets in their assignments and they aim to hit them, regardless of what they are.

Companies enable this behavior by not recognizing that they need to set metrics that are specific and appropriate. If you want your product managers to be marketers then measure them on their ability to penetrate markets; if you want them to be strategic then set strategy-based metrics.

These metrics are a fundamental part of the hiring process that companies tend to overlook. Unfortunately, this mistake is not an easy problem to solve because once the metrics are changed you may realize that you don't have the right people to meet them. With new job metrics comes a required change in behavior that not all product managers can provide.

7. *Inadequate Processes for Developing and Vetting Product Plans*

Planning is a discipline and a process, not an event. A lot of companies talk about it but few commit wholly to it by saying, "We want plans from our product managers and we're going to vet those plans appropriately to measure their viability."

An organization that is truly dedicated to planning has a process in place to review plans and to determine which resources to apply to support them. They also make sure these plans are consistent with corporate targets.

In order to effectively evaluate product plans, there needs to be clear criteria, priorities and objectives. What are the impacts of the plan and how will that affect the organization? Unfortunately, planning in some organizations is considered an event—something lumped in with budgets at the end of the year or something that is driven by a need to justify a predetermined course of action.

Planning is an evergreen process because the markets change continually. A planning discipline enables the company to know where it is going and enables product managers to analyze and assess plans based on dynamics in existing, emerging and adjacent markets for each product on an ongoing basis.

What are the kinds of things you are going to do as a company to significantly change how you do business? And how are you going to enter markets and accomplish your goals there? Is there a framework in place in your organization for providing the answer to that question? Has a formalized process been put in place to effectively assess product plans and strategies? Does it assess the product line from a life cycle management perspective? Are trade-offs being made and adhered to?

8. *Inability to Innovate*

A common complaint from presidents and CEOs is that they don't feel like they're getting enough product innovation. They are concerned that new product ideas are being driven mostly from engineering and R&D rather than the market. They don't understand why product management isn't leading product strategy.

What's missing and driving most presidents and CEOs crazy is solid and consistent market data. Market research, including voice-of-the-customer information, is essential to product innovation. What we find is that much of the market research that companies conduct is done from a macro point of view for purposes of corporate strategy and corporate branding. The information that is obtained from the data is either too macro for product managers to extrapolate down to the product level or, worse, the data is not shared with them at all!

Other research tends to be focused on product definition as part of the new product-development process. In this case, the voice of the customer is ascertained primarily to define features and functionality for a specific product and isn't repeatedly gathered. Customer satisfaction surveys put a finger on the pulse of current customers and should be issued frequently.

Unfortunately, even when this research is conducted, it's done in isolation with no connection to an overarching strategy; data does not get disseminated effectively and any action based on the findings focus on short-term activities rather than long-term strategic initiatives.

What is lacking is a focus on data acquisition at "ground

level" that product managers can use to spot market trends and changing customer requirements within existing, adjacent and emerging market segments.

A market-focused organization continually studies existing markets, adjacent markets and new markets with an eye toward getting in front of the customer to understand the issues that are impacting them. This approach is about bringing real value to the markets and that's a big shift for companies that have traditionally been internally focused.

The change to a market-focused organization begins with executive leadership that gets ingrained into the culture of the company over time. It becomes a significant aspect of how an organization operates and evaluates business opportunities.

Conversely, changing to a market-focused organization does not mean expanding market research budgets and resources. It means recognizing all information coming into the organization as being "market information" suitable for use by product managers and others in developing appropriate strategies. It also means providing the infrastructure to effectively and efficiently disseminate the information to all parts of the organization, including product management.

CHAPTER 6

Establishing a Baseline

Every organization, no matter its mission, faces the challenge of using resources as efficiently as possible. How a company uses resources says a lot about its efficiency and also about how clear a mission it has for the future. Product managers are a resource.

Product managers, as we've discussed, can be a driving force in a company. They can set the direction if they truly know the market and are adept at planning how to take advantage of it. But getting the most from product managers really begins at the top.

In the two previous chapters, we've discussed the common mistakes that both product managers and their organizations make. And while it's easy to identify some of the more common mistakes these two entities might make, it's a little more difficult to tell an organization what they might do to fix them—especially because doing so sometimes requires executive management to change their thinking completely.

One of the most common challenges we see in the industrial or business-to-business sectors is the decision-making process that management goes through in figuring out how best to use product managers. How people—and the organizations they work for—define the product management role can vary greatly. This disconnect in the understanding of the role of a PM can affect any level of an organization's operations. And it leads to a few questions you should ask yourself right now:

- Do the product managers in your organization really have the right metrics to measure success?
- Where do the product managers reside in the organizational structure? If they are in engineering or sales, get them out!
- Do the leaders in the organization even know what they want out of their product managers?

The reality is that different companies have different requirements for their product management positions. The answers to the above questions will depend on what you need from your product managers, except for the last one; that question needs to be a definitive "yes."

There is no room for indecision when it comes to the product management positions. The managers in these positions should be capable of long-term planning, but first they need a charter that is clear and concise.

Getting to a place where your organization can establish an

unequivocal set of guidelines for its product managers means first examining the current guidelines and the results they are producing. If your product managers are not fulfilling your hopes for them, begin by looking at their goals and objectives.

Getting a Baseline

The first step for any organization that hopes to improve a process is to take a baseline reading of where they are in terms of strengths and weaknesses. The process is no different when it comes to product management.

The first part of determining whether or not your organization is operating a high-performance culture of product management is to ask questions. Sometimes these questions are uncomfortable or outside the normal scope of thinking in the organization, but they're the only way to establish a clear picture of where the organization stands.

These questions may include:

- What are the strengths and weaknesses of the people in the role of product manager?
- What is expected of them?
- Does product management work as a cohesive group?
- Where do most product managers come from in your organization?
- Does your company have a farm system to develop product managers?
- Are your product managers capable of being generalists and specialists?
- Is the organization a planning-oriented, market-focused one?
- Does the leadership have the resources and willingness to change?

- Do you have the right IT systems to support your product managers?
- Can product managers get the right information when they need it?
- Does the organization adequately and effectively disseminate information?
- Is the organization's planning effective?
- How connected is product management to corporate strategic planning?
- Does the organization even do strategic planning at the corporate level?
- Is the strategic plan consistently referred to and what effect does it have on lower-level planning?

Perhaps the most important of any of these questions is: does your company leadership have the resources and willingness to change? Without a definitive "yes," your organization is dead in the water. Any major change in the systems of a large industrial company is going to require resources, time and perhaps forced changes in personnel.

While the intention to change is admirable, these kinds of changes are not possible if implemented in the middle of an organization or by one small group somewhere in the bowels of the company. There must be a clear message sent to the members of the organization that product managers will interact with other divisions in a new way, that a major change is expected and supported, and that planning is now going to be required and expected.

What most of these questions come back to is: ***does management understand the concept of product management?***

Product managers are a reflection of their organizations. If they are supported by an organization that is proactive, not reactive, they will likely try and be the same (key word: try).

If your company is suffering from the "Following the Competition" mistake from Chapter 4 then you may want to consider reevaluating your planning process as a part of improving your product management setup.

Making the leap from reactive to proactive involves finding and establishing people in the product management positions who understand what the market wants. As we've discussed already, finding people to match what is desired by the organization is not so easy. Bridging the gap means going back to basics. And that begins with knowing what you want and then exploring what you have. The following questions will help you hone in on what exactly you need for your company.

1. What exactly does your organization want from the product management position?

This comes back to what is ultimately the purpose of this book: leveraging resources and making the most of what the PM is doing.

Every company is different, but if the leadership recognizes where they are as a company and what their needs are, they'll be able to make a better determination of what role the product managers will play, how many different roles they need and what level of authority those people will have.

Unfortunately, we've seen that most companies don't understand what's involved in an effective product management organization and how it fits within their overall business structures. The executive leadership says they want to meet certain objectives, but they sometimes don't know how that translates into a mandate for their product managers. What's more, they apply the wrong metrics for measuring success as they've defined it.

Listed below are the required attributes for any good PM. As part of establishing your baseline, you need to look at these attributes and make sure that you've written a job description for your product managers that focus on them. Then determine if you've hired people who have them or can grow into them and that you've established metrics for measuring these qualities.

Also, as a part of a baseline, these attributes will answer the question: do we have the right people in the role?

It's important to look at the people in the role of PM and remember that they should be linked as a product management group or team.

- **Business Owners**: Product managers need to have some fundamental knowledge of how to run a product line as a business. They should understand revenue and profitability, and how that contributes to overall company objectives. Product managers are often talked about as mini-CEOs or GMs and really they have to be able to understand the financials of the business. So, are the PM roles in your organization populated by people with these attributes?
- **Marketers**: This does not refer to marketing communications or writing ad copy. This is about understanding the marketplace and the customer sets that have needs for products or services. Do your product managers

understand how needs differ in customers so that they can find out where the value lies? Are they differentiating between market segments and do they understand that they are different for a reason, and that they need to leverage those differences? For example, customers have different needs and may even be different in how they buy. The strategy for dealing with a set of customers that are price-oriented, commodity-driven, low-cost and no-frills is a much different strategy than one applied to value-oriented customers that are less price-sensitive. Do your product managers understand that, and can they communicate this to management?

- **Good Strategists**: Product managers must understand all four Ps of the marketing mix. Beyond product and feature sets, they must also be thinking about and directing pricing and discount strategies, must understand sales and channel issues, and must be capable of product positioning and promotion. They need to be capable of developing the key strategies required to gain a sustainable competitive advantage.
- **Planners**: Product managers need to prioritize their own resources and plans and have long-term vision. They are most effective when they provide focus and direction for the organization so that the product line is being developed in an efficient way.

Are your product managers a good match for the criteria listed above? More importantly, is this what you want and expect from your product managers? Once you've answered these questions, begin to look at your organization.

Industrial companies tend to be sales- and product-driven. Engineering and development are their fortes and while most of the organizations we work with have very good products and have been near the top of the market space, they tend to adopt the *Field of Dreams* attitude we talked about earlier, depending on the product to draw customers.

This inward focus often leads to confusion about what role the product managers should play. After all, if your organization is built around a culture that is tactical and product-focused in nature, then it stands to reason that the position of PM will be artificially limited in scope and will be that of a *project* manager rather than a product champion.

2. Where are you finding your product management talent?

Industrial product management requires technical proficiency and knowledge of how the products are used, so it stands to reason that product development and sales would be logical areas to search for PM candidates. However, this comes with some caveats. First, product managers that come from R&D tend to define markets from a product perspective. Product managers that come from development tend to focus on what technology can be leveraged in a product rather than what technology is really necessary to fit the customer's needs. It's the tail wagging the dog and it seldom produces the best results.

Second, product managers that come from sales tend to define markets based on specific customers and product requirements based on the latest complaint or lost business. If sales-oriented product managers rely solely on feedback from a single customer, the result is a lot of one-off changes and custom products that may not be commercially acceptable. Without the associated balance of the other aspects of the role, the tendency is to make small, individual, incremental changes rather than innovative product decisions that can help the company dominate the market.

Third, how much marketing competency is in your product management organization? "We'll bring in product specialists and teach them marketing!" Have you ever heard that before? Maybe you've even said it yourself. How did that work out for you? It's not as easy as it sounds. Since product management is a marketing position, it may make sense to hire individuals with marketing skills and teach them about the product. One thing companies do well is educate customers and employees about the products and services they sell.

Finally, product managers need to be both generalists and specialists. It's difficult to get pure specialists to become market-focused because it's not the way they are programmed. Being too married to one mode of thinking will hamstring a PM and keep him from being effective. There are plenty of effective product managers that have come from sales and engineering. As long as your people are flexible and adaptable, and have the aptitude for the other aspects required for the role, including business strategy, planning, marketing and finance, they can grow into the role and become an "intrepreneur," which is our term for someone who exhibits all of the leadership qualities we look for in a product manager.

3. Where do the product managers reside in your organization?

Deciding where product managers reside in an organization can become a problem. By positioning product managers poorly, an organization misses the opportunity to make it a strategic position.

The product manager is responsible for bringing balance to three fundamental agendas: business objectives, market needs and company capabilities. In their most formidable role, product managers strike the balance between potentially competing agendas, specifically the inherent conflict between managing operational costs and delivering the appropriate breadth of products and services to meet market needs. So, what does this have to do with where product managers reside, you say? Everything.

To start with, product managers should report to marketing because product management is first and foremost a marketing function. Second, product management should have its own seat at the management table independent of other functional areas. Many companies have product management located in a specific functional area, such as sales or, in some cases, even operations or product development. Unfortunately, when product management is located within one of these areas, it tends to be seen as a support function rather than a strategic function. It's critical that product management be treated as equal to other groups within marketing.

If product management is located in the sales organization, product managers are typically used for sales and customer-support activities, shepherding projects that are driven by the sales force. Conversely, when product management is part of the product-development or engineering function, product managers are viewed more as project managers limited to internal management of project milestones and other more tactical activities.

The reality is that they need to be at a peer level with each of these functions as well as a peer to operations. Product managers in a peer relationship will provide significant value balancing the competing needs of the sales force with the development desires of research and development, and the production-efficiency requirements driven by operations.

Where the product management function resides within an organization indicates how product management is perceived in the organization and inherently sets the level of expectation regardless of what is being said throughout the company. Sometimes titles and positions mean more than intentions.

4. What roles do your product managers perform?

An organization's maturity will have a lot to do with where the product managers are positioned. Many younger companies ask more of their product managers as do-it-all role players. The more products a company has and the more markets it's involved in, the more likely they will want an entrepreneurial business manager and strategist. Usually, as companies grow, the role becomes more relevant and strategic in nature. At least that's what many companies want as they grow.

5. How linked are the product managers to the strategic planning process?

Corporations typically create plans for three- to five-year hori-
zons, and yet we see product managers frequently left out of
this process. Product managers shouldn't just have information passed down to them; they should be linked to the process
so that there is a two-way flow of information.

As mentioned earlier, there is a need for product managers to be involved in the strategic process because corporate
strategy informs product decisions, and product and market
information compiled by product managers can inform corporate strategic thinking.

If there is a good flow of information, then the product
managers will be able to use that to align the product-line
strategies to the corporate strategies. When changes to the
corporate strategies are made, they need to be communicated
so that everyone understands what's driving the strategy.

At the portfolio and product level, it is critical that the right
infrastructure is in place to support a disciplined approach to
planning for all product managers. Having this infrastructure
allows them to interface with the organization in a uniform
way. It also ensures that product managers work in concert with
one another when it comes to developing strategic plans. After
all, in most companies, product managers are vying against
one another for the same financial and human resources. It
stands to reason that product management should evaluate
and make trade-offs within their own functional area before
going out to the rest of the organization.

In our interactions with organizations large and small,
we've seen as few as three and as many as hundreds of product
managers operating with no formal process for this type of

interaction. Most are talking to each other on a less formalized basis, but what happens in these interactions is not uniform. Each pairing is trying to do something different, which may not be in the best interests of the organization.

The fallout from this lack of communication is that the rest of the organization looks at product management and says, "They're not operating as one front." We've even had one of our clients' executive managers say of his organization's product management, "They're all acting like sub-contractors."

To be most effective, product managers need to be linked to the strategic planning process and must have a formalized process within their own organization to properly assess and vet product plans. Without that, the rest of organization won't pay attention to them because they won't have credibility.

6. Are there specific metrics aligned with the product manager accountabilities?

Most every company we have talked to has metrics based around tactical activities, like how many products the PM gets into the pipeline per year and how effective product managers are at getting products launched. When an organization puts metrics like those in place, they force product managers to focus on internal activities and manage their products tactically.

We will give further attention to establishing these metrics in later chapters, but for now it's important for you to examine how exactly you are measuring success from your product managers. Are you focusing on the efficacy of their three- and five-year plans? Are you keeping track of how your organization's products are placed against the competition? Are you measuring PM success based on product acceptance in the market?

7. Do you have a development and succession plan for product management?

Prior to becoming an effective product manager, every manager needs training and work experience in the areas that are going to play a role in the position. When scouting talent in the organization for these positions, there must be a focus on determining if a candidate has the capability to grow into the larger functions.

Most of the product managers we see come from the product side. They have technical knowledge and have also had interaction with customers, so they seem like good candidates. The same question remains, though: can they develop into strategists and be externally focused?

Most companies have not designed a good system to develop and promote product managers and to fit them in to various roles. Inevitably this causes problems for the organization when a PM is promoted or leaves. The void created is larger than the existing skill sets available within the product management function and you're back to square one.

Ask yourself if you have a development plan in place that builds the competencies required for each level of product manager. Are you aligning the skill sets and capabilities of individuals to leverage strengths and maximize performance? Have you created a succession plan that allows you to quickly and effectively back fill and reload rather than constantly rebuild your product management organization?

There is a tremendous advantage for your organization if

you take the time to cultivate, nurture and grow your product managers. B2B companies invest little time and resources in their PMs but expect the role to somehow evolve. The technical complexity of industrial products coupled with the knowledge of the markets cannot easily be replaced, which puts product lines at risk.

With a clearly defined order of succession, it is easier to hire, promote and develop your resources. With a formalized plan in place, you can eliminate stopgap hires, make product-line transitions easier and develop a more proficient product management competency.

8. Does your company have the information infrastructure in place to maximize the PM role?

Timely information is critical for product managers. If a PM is going to act as a business owner, then he needs the same kind of information that the business owner would receive.

When examining your infrastructure as part of your baseline, ask yourself this: Is there a way for reports and data to be gathered easily so that the product managers can process and structure information quickly? Can the product managers track sales activities in the channels of distribution? Can they analyze revenue and gross profits for the product line and their entire portfolio?

In many companies product managers cannot do these things. It is not acceptable to make your product managers go through a long exercise to acquire the data. They also should not have to then reformat the information in order to present it in a way they need to. Inadequate report capabilities are probably the single biggest reason for information voids we see and, in today's business environment, information has to be at a push of a button so that informed decisions can be made quickly.

Part of the problem is that many organizations don't know what product managers want in the way of information. Some of the communication gap may originate with the product managers and some of it may come from the organization's having never asked the product managers what information they need. Regardless of the reason, consistent and accurate information is a must if you want your product managers to make informed and fact-based product and market decisions.

As you can tell from the format of this chapter, establishing a baseline requires quite a bit of querying. But it is necessary to understanding why product managers are not meeting the expectations of their management.

Without outside consultation and expertise, establishing a baseline may be a limited process but it should at least involve an audit and assessment that addresses two areas: planning and systems. These are the areas that dictate the product management position's success and are the areas we believe are most important to eliminate any problems.

CHAPTER 7

Designing Your Organization

Once an organization's baseline is set, the next step is to start fixing what is broken. While identifying an existing problem in an organization is fairly straightforward and can be done through data collection or an examination of metrics, the cleanup is often messier and more time-consuming. And so it is with putting the right people into the product management positions in an organization.

When instituting changes, especially personnel changes, the goal should always be the same: to improve the performance of the position so that the work produced is in line with the organizational goals.

Sometimes changes are made to minimize labor costs, and while that is a valid business decision, the changes outlined in this chapter are aimed at restructuring the product management positions in an organization that is looking for a more visionary, strategic and market-focused performance from its product managers. Finding people with these talents often means paying more, not less. The payoffs, though, are worth it.

Chapters 4 and 5 examined the common mistakes product managers and their organizations make in creating and managing the position. Chapter 6 asked a series of questions about what kind of people are in the PM positions at your organization and whether or not your organization is sufficiently supporting them in their work.

The next step is to act on the answers to those questions.

I recognize that most of you already have a product management organization in place and therefore do not have the luxury of starting with a clean sheet of paper. However, don't let it dissuade you from looking at ways to modify the organization in order to optimize its performance.

Putting Your House in Order

Let form follow function. For whatever reason, be it personal or financial, many organizations refuse to acknowledge that their product managers are not suited for the job. It's the square-peg, round-hole syndrome and it's deadly to optimization.

To alleviate this problem, the director of product management should start by defining the structure of the product management organization based on the level of complexity in the product lines and the markets. Once the structure is identified, roles can be defined. Then you can look at the resources to determine if the people you have can fit the roles. The chances are good that you will require many different product management roles depending on the size and sophistication of your organization. Let's look at creating the structure first.

Step 1: Create the organizational structure.

While some people are not meant for high-level product management—being business owners, marketers, planners and strategists—some are capable of performing the role if it is specifically designed to be tactical and at a lower level.

Many organizations have the need for, and room for, multiple strata of product management. It is not uncommon to see an organization decide to divide the duties of its product managers based on experience and ability. As long as the roles are clearly defined, this kind of system can work.

As discussed in the previous chapter, some organizations leave strategic planning to the CEO or COO. In these cases, the product management position is bound to be more tactical. If that is the case with your organization, then a decision needs to be made as to what each PM should be doing. What the product managers are ultimately tasked with will depend on several factors.

In larger companies with a requirement for strategic thinking, it may be desirable to at least have someone coordinating activities with marketing and sales to establish messaging or value propositions. This level of product management may also involve developing marketing strategies with outside agencies.

Multi-million- to multi-billion-dollar companies will deal

with more distinct markets and so the product managers will likely be required to develop product-line strategies and to act as business owners. Typically we find in B2B and industrial organizations that this competency is hard to find because these organizations deal with a very technical sales process. For this reason, it is always good in the industrial marketplace to have a blend of people that are both product and market savvy—especially because, in these environments, product managers are often called on by the sales organization to discuss issues with customers, and that means being comfortable in outside business interactions.

However the product managers in your organization are organized, the hierarchy will be informed by your company's evolution. It's okay to stratify your product managers, as long as the roles are made clear. You can have coordinators who do competitive analysis and market analysis, and tactical product managers who handle issues with engineering and marketing to make sure part numbers are being labeled correctly. The larger picture can be left to the visionaries who decide what to do with the product portfolio.

Step 2: Define the responsibilities and metrics for each PM.

Once you've established which roles are needed, it is necessary to clearly define the functional responsibilities for each. We find that defining the job descriptions from the most strategic to least strategic is the best way to begin. Start by identifying the key result areas or key performance indicators that you feel each job responsibility should have.

Example: If you have decided that you require a product manager in a highly strategic role, you may determine that this individual will be responsible for managing an entire product portfolio. As the portfolio manager, they may have the responsibility for product-line revenue and profitability, as well as staff management responsibilities. Given the nature of this role, you may identify key result areas as:

1. Portfolio Management
2. Product-Line Planning
3. Employee Management and Development

Establishing key result areas enables both product managers and their managers to have a clear direction and focus on functional activities that are most appropriate to the role. Once the key result areas are defined, the next step is to enumerate specific critical tasks for each key result area that will guide the product manager in performing the role.

Example: Depending on how you define the portfolio management key result area, specific critical tasks might include:

1. Monitor the business performance of the existing product line against company goals.
2. Review and refine the product portfolio to achieve business results.
3. Provide requirements for product enhancements, new product developments and end-of-life strategies based on market-segment opportunities.
4. Coordinate PM activities within the product portfolio to minimize product conflicts and

leverage product synergies to meet company expectations.

5. Work with managers in other key business functions to maximize product-line profitability, inventory levels and production forecasts.

Finally, you can assign specific performance metrics aligned to the critical tasks to measure performance.

All product managers will not have the same roles, job descriptions and job functions, so it is important to develop specific key result areas, critical tasks and performance metrics based on the role each will perform.

Generally we have found that roles fit into three levels or categories for product managers:

1. **Support Role**: In smaller companies, business owners or general managers are the people really doing the market or product strategies. Smaller organizations that are flatter generally reflect this way of thinking and product managers in these companies are usually in a "support role." When this is the case, the product managers are more likely to be product-focused and tactically oriented. They will execute the day-to-day product activities and typically work very closely with operations and other internal functions to handle part numbers, data sheets, bills of materials, etc.— activities that are very product-oriented and internally focused.

2. **Coordinators**: Product managers in the coordinator role are primarily involved in

problem-solving with a limited role in strategy development. These product managers may do the product implementation and execution but are also more involved in marketing tasks, including market research. Coordinators may take on more duties and responsibilities than the support-role product managers, but they are still primarily focused on internal aspects of product development and launch.

3. **Executives**: Product managers at this level take on the role of business owners, strategists, marketers and planners, and are asked to be product champions. They are literally creating the strategies as they relate to the markets they serve and the business objectives the organization has. Product managers in this role may even have coordinator and support product managers working for them, allocating resources more effectively between tactical day-to-day activities and strategic long-term activities.

Step 3: Align the resources to the roles.

Though certain unhappy marriages between senior management and a PM can be resolved amicably, there are times when divorce is the best way. Some people are more comfortable in tactical positions that focus on product development or project management.

We've encountered many product managers who are fantastically capable in a technical aspect, but incapable of performing the marketing requirements of the position. The PM must be able to deal with customers and envision the market as a whole. Being a talented generalist is important in the PM position, so specialists are better moved elsewhere.

Caution must be used in the evaluation of each PM for several reasons, not least of which an understanding that oftentimes it is the organization is that is pushing tactical metrics onto a position that requires strategic thinking and planning. If that is the case, then new metrics need to implemented before a true evaluation of performance can be made.

Selecting the Right Individuals

One of the more common questions we hear is, "Where do we go to find our product management talent?"

A good first step is to determine how technical your product or service is. If you determine that technical expertise is the most significant requirement for your product managers then it might be advantageous to search for product management talent from within your ranks.

If, however, you determine that product knowledge can be taught and that marketing expertise and an ability to observe and understand user and usage factors is more important, you may want to consider looking outside of your organization. The reasons are many, but the most important is the way in which product management has evolved in industrial and business-to-business companies.

Unlike in the fast-moving consumer-goods sector, product management in industrial companies grew primarily from an internal view that someone was needed to manage the tactical activities around the product line.

As industrial companies continue to evolve, managers are coming to the realization that the PM role needs to be more externally focused. Given this realization, managers are recognizing that it is increasingly necessary to find candidates that have strong market aptitude and marketing skill sets and that are capable of learning the product and its technical aspects to effectively relate them to market needs.

If you truly want to develop a product management organization that is market-oriented, it is essential to look for individuals with marketing skills and aptitude. For a number of companies, especially those that have been product- and technically focused in their hiring practices, this often means looking outward.

We've dealt with managers in industrial companies who get frustrated time and again when they choose individuals with technical expertise to be product managers. They falsely believe they can teach these product managers marketing, only to realize that marketing is more of an aptitude than a skill. Or, worse yet, the company never finds the time or resources to provide adequate marketing training to new product managers.

Personality, Competency and Experience

When you look for PM candidates, consider these skills, knowledge and abilities:

1. **Personality**: Product managers interface with a varied assortment of people, both within the organization and without. They need to be

tactful and work in cross-functional teams. Because they have few direct-report staff, they must borrow resources and people without stepping on too many toes.

Any new hire needs the ability to influence the process and the people. That means finding effective communicators and planners. Can your candidates get their point across and influence people? If not, they won't succeed as a product manager.

Are your candidates levelheaded? Product managers can't be sensitive to changing moods because of the different personalities they'll face on a day-to-day basis. They have to influence well and that means adjusting tactics and demeanor based on their counterpart in either their own organization or at an existing client.

2. **Competency**: Being up-to-speed on the specifications of a product, the market conditions of the day or the topics customers care about is vital because credibility is a huge factor in how well a PM is regarded. Planning, organization, business acumen, salesmanship, leadership: these are all crucial in being competent.

3. **Experience**: The real value product managers have for a company is not development or sales, but the understanding of the markets and competitors. That's why it is so important to be a marketer when it comes to seeing the playing field. Blending that knowledge with an understanding of the company's capabilities

and objectives requires experience in multiple fields. Product line and portfolio management are not positions for recent grads without experience. Being in charge of a product portfolio takes wisdom and tact.

Growing Managers

One of the biggest problems companies have is developing bench strength in the product management organization to compensate for turnover. Industrial companies, normally weaker in marketing competency than their retail counterparts, can begin to develop marketing and product management as a core competency with the right planning.

First: Create a pathway for growth into the role of PM by deliberately increasing responsibility for lower-level product managers. Even if lower-level product managers don't fill vacant senior PM positions, they can move into other parts of the organization and contribute their acquired skills. If they want to move into marketing or sales, they will already have some of those competencies.

Second: Push each product manager to shore up weaknesses through mentorships with more experienced managers. By developing your product managers completely, you empower them to move into positions such as division manager, CEO and other levels.

Third: Establish specific strata for advancing product managers so that each has an incentive to grow with your organization. Product managers are sometimes groomed for division management and company management in many of the consumer-product industries. Many industrial companies don't have a way to create that competency, no pathway for growing product managers. Having a nice mix of positions gives prospective product managers a chance to migrate and learn all three levels of the job.

CHAPTER 8

Putting the Systems in Place to Support Your People

Once your product management house is in order, you can begin to work on the other factors that enhance product management and industrial-marketing success, namely, building or solidifying the support infrastructure and interrelationships between product management and the rest of the your organization.

Keys to Successful Implementation

Find a Champion

First, you have to have a champion whose responsibility it is to run the overall product management organization. Building the bench, developing the talent and creating a growth path for individuals who join product management is critical to long term success.

Why is this so important? Our experience shows that many companies have relatively flat product management organizations with most or all of the product managers responsible for all activities tactical and strategic, regardless of skill level and capabilities. Nearly every time a PM position opens up, it creates a void in product-line consistency. In the vast majority of cases, managers find themselves scrambling to find someone to fill the position. During this time, other product managers are asked to fill in as caretakers while managing their own product lines.

The end result is a lack of focus on not one but two or more product lines. There must be constant assessment of the "who" and "how" of product management and marketing. The "who" is the individuals and attributes that are required to fill the roles; the "how" is the skills, knowledge and abilities required to successfully perform the roles.

Without a development system, the results are predictable: every time a new PM comes on board, the learning process has to start at square one, which is time-consuming and ineffective. Product-line focus is lost; revenues and profits suffer; product managers and their peers get frustrated; and the organization loses confidence in the product management's ability to lead. Think about how many times you've experienced this scenario and how difficult it is to overcome.

We've worked with numerous clients that have taken this concept of product management and marketing competency and put it into practice by developing marketing centers of excellence within their organizations. We've also seen organizations that have elevated marketing and product management functions to peer level with other functional areas as a means of establishing them as leadership positions with a seat at the table.

Define the Rules of Engagement

We've spoken about this several times in the book, but it bears repeating: once you have a written set of expectations and metrics for the role of product manager, define the rules of engagement for the rest of the organization.

Product managers don't manage the people who complete all of the individual tasks that comprise product management, but they still need to get people to work the process for them. If others in the organization aren't told how they should work with the product managers, then you end up with failures, and product success is everyone's responsibility. All functional areas have a hand in how successful a product is. But what role do they need to play? Does your organization know? Does each functional manager know? Clearly defined rules go a long way toward overcoming the problems inherent in cross-functional organizations.

Use Product Manager Market Knowledge to Inform Others in the Organization

Product managers need to be the voice of the market. Product planning becomes more relevant in all aspects with this information being shared by multiple departments. It also helps to define which enhancements should go into existing products and what new products are needed. Rationalization of new product lines is made easier when the product managers are fueling the process with accurate market information.

With full engagement between departments, each department can set up goals based on the market knowledge of the product managers. That's not to say they control this process, but they can be a big influence in getting everyone aligned to the marketplace.

Shifting the focus of an organization from being reactive to being a life-cycle-centric organization means understanding where each product is in its own life cycle. Product can inform corporate-level decisions based on how the product is sitting in the marketplace.

If a PM knows that a product is going to be obsolete in the marketplace, she can inform engineering, product development, sales and marketing. She can also make recommendations for what new products need to be added to the mix by looking at existing products to see what needs to be enhanced or can stay the same.

This process of structured interaction helps in operations and resource allocation. With life cycles as the focus of planning, it makes it more relevant and shifts the product-development direction onto the product managers so that they can feed new ideas and requirements into the pipeline.

Every department in matrix-based companies has objectives. Sales has to increase revenues, operations has to make the company more efficient and so on. The problem is that these goals are set vertically but are not necessarily connected to broader objectives that cover the entire company. Your company will get a lot more bang for the buck if all departments are driving toward objectives tied to the market for their products and services.

Product managers can play a beneficial role in all of this. When they provide focus and direction, they contribute to everyone's success.

Uniformity Is Key

Once your product managers have access to information, the reports they generate as a result must be based on an established system that provides for uniformity and a strong vetting process. At this point in the process, it is prudent to ask several questions of your organization:

- Do the product managers and their employees use the same documents and terminology to express their plans to a larger audience?
- Are they vetting the plans they produce?
- Are long-term plans looked at in a specific way based on relevant criteria?
- Is there a system in place that allows for progress reviews on a quarterly basis?

These questions are important because they help establish a common language for reporting ideas and a set of benchmarks for measuring how well a plan has lived up to its predictions. Again, these are long-term plans and so they require long-term assessments. And it is those assessments by which a PM should be judged.

Product managers should be in a position to deliver that kind of value through plans and they should be given the tools to create those plans. Others divisions in the organization likely have tools and templates, so why not product managers?

With some of these questions answered and subsequent plans set in motion, the process of building a culture of high-performance product management has begun in earnest.

CHAPTER 9

Strategic Product Planning As a Discipline

If the PM is truly going to be a leader in your organization, then his plans need to reflect that reality. Effective strategic product planning is not an event that takes place only when a product is being phased out or introduced; it is a process that follows the entire life cycle of the product.

Strategic planning involves a great deal of assessment that takes into account market conditions and corporate objectives. It must weigh the beginning, middle and end of a product's life and is really the heart of what a PM does. Most of the characteristics we attribute to good product managers are based around their ability to formulate and defend long-term strategic plans.

Strategic planning, if done correctly, should be what drives the day-to-day operations at the product line, product portfolio and operational levels. By creating a culture of high-performance product management, your organization can depend on solid leadership and vision versus the if-we-build-it-they-will-come mentality.

The consequence, of course, for not instilling these principles into an organization is that products are created in a vacuum versus through an informed assessment of the market. What's more, without vision, there is no way to vet opportunities that come from sales, engineering or marketing.

Because of their constant interaction with customers, sales will likely have ideas about what the product should provide based on the feedback they receive. But how will the PM know if those ideas are catering to one client or to ten? How will he or she know if the opportunities placed in front of him or her by sales are worth expending precious resources?

They will know if they have a road map through which to vet all opportunities. By having a one- to three-year plan established and under regular review, the PM can examine an opportunity in the context of existing markets and can even measure the risks involved against predicted future market conditions.

So What Do These Strategic Plans Look Like?

First and foremost, any plan must be written. That may seem a redundant statement, but you would be surprised how many corporations have no written plans that detail their next one to three years of product-portfolio management.

There are a lot of reasons certain companies operate without an agreed-upon, long-term plan, but the result is usually the same: a lack of direction and inefficient use of resources in the organization. Operating without a plan also results in product strategies that don't align with corporate objectives.

Next, product line and portfolio plans should be multi-generational and include a comprehensive vision of new product development, product enhancements and extensions, and end-of-life strategies. Planning, if fully instilled in the corporate structure and emphasized as a discipline to be practiced by all managers and leaders, is what sets the leading companies apart from those that are reactionary. Being surprised by your markets is often a result of poor analysis by product managers. It can also be the result of an organization that isn't listening to what the product managers are saying about the markets.

Keep It Fact-Based

One of the first questions we hear when proposing a new method of product planning is "How long should the plans be?" While we don't recommend that the plans challenge the length of a Russian novel, we do encourage product managers to make sure that their plans address all areas of product development and launch, and that they be fact-based.

A certain level of judgment is required when creating a plan, but that judgment will only be persuasive if based on real trends and figures. With organizations of all stripes looking to save money, the allocation of resources will become a battleground for product managers in the future. Leading the way in these situations will require solid planning and a thorough understanding of the markets in which a given product competes.

Finally, plans should bring the market perspective into full view and provide focus and direction for the corporation.

They should be aligned with the corporate strategies and business objectives in a way that informs both leadership and any functional area of the company that might be involved in implementing parts of the plan.

When we say they should bring market perspective into full view, we mean the plan should articulate the different markets and market segments that are in play. The product manager should be able to illustrate how the markets are different and how the differences in the markets inform the need for different marketing mix strategies. These plans should include the following market information:

1. Any market segments to be targeted
2. Segment size and share data
3. Segment trends and emerging opportunities
4. Key segment differences
5. Competitive assessment of existing products in the marketplace

Product plans must align the product strategies to the markets that they are intended to serve. Without due diligence, business product strategies are rudderless ships.

What's In It for the Company?

So how does all of this planning and effort move your organization closer to what you're trying to accomplish, namely, increased revenue and profits, operational efficiency and increased market share? By acting as a road map.

Product plans should be considered prospectuses that

organizations use to consider where and how they want to invest their resources. Ultimately, the product plan must include the financial justification for each recommendations, including:

1. Market forecasts
2. Sales and revenue forecasts
3. Pricing and margin analysis
4. Contribution analysis
5. Cost/benefit analysis
6. ROI and breakeven analysis

Product managers must provide clear financial justification for the product and portfolio strategies they present. Without a sound "business justification," product managers will not gain access to the resources of the organization, including the sales channels, marketing resources and operational resources required to successfully manage their product lines.

Does It Link to Corporate Strategy?

What we normally see in industrial or B2B companies is a great deal of top-down movement in the flow of information and planning. But we rarely see it get filtered down to the product managers. From a planning standpoint, that can be poisonous.

The strategic plans created by product managers drive the business and, as such, also act as a measure of whether or not the product managers are getting what they need, like resources and funding. Because this is the PM presenting his or her case to management, any disparity in the flow of information becomes immediately apparent.

The portfolio planning we see is often done without a link to the corporate strategic goals of the organization, and sometimes the strategic objectives aren't even known by the product managers. The result is plans that are inconsistent with the business' goals.

When that happens, the organization has already wasted resources by having product managers and their support staff create plans that will be of little relevance. Not only have the product managers been out of focus on their plan, but it also implies that the product managers are examining the market in a way that isn't as targeted as it could be given more guidance from the upper echelons of the organization.

Portfolio planning is about the big picture. Whatever the planning horizon is, the product and portfolio plans should be on the same timetable. Based on their ability to understand the marketplace, product managers ought to be able to put together some high-level strategies that take into account the facts on the ground so they can project what they think will happen. This planning must also be done with an understanding that the plans are not static. That means that as new information comes into play, the product managers can look at the plans and either validate them or adjust them based on new information.

What's the Long-Term Vision?

Perhaps the most important aspect of any plan is the end goal. Where do you want to invest and where do you want to divest? You can't assume that every market will be viable forever. Are the markets you serve today going to be the markets you serve tomorrow? The portfolio plan should also include how the organization is aligned with the markets, industries and applications it serves.

One of the great benefits of a process of constant assessment is the opportunity to craft a portfolio that is at the very crest of the market wave. This emphasis on assessments in advance of developments provides an avenue for recommendations to be made so the organization can get ahead of what the market is doing. This provides the organization direction, which ultimately is what a plan is for.

The strategic product or portfolio plan provides a road map that grants guidance based on the same knowledge product managers use to vet ideas as they come in. Product managers should constantly be asking the question, "What do I need to be doing with my product line?"

It is the product manager's playbook that says, "This is the business that I own, these are the products that constitute the business, these are the markets we're focused on and here is the revenue and profit we expect to achieve." It becomes the centerpiece of his or her decision-making process.

For product managers, the road map enables them to act as gatekeepers, using the plan as a basis for decision-making by vetting new opportunities and ideas against the plan.

They can ask, "Does the idea or opportunity fit with the goals and objectives of this product line and does it target the markets we've chosen to target?" If yes, they might accept the product idea. And if it doesn't meet these requirements, they can ask if it will serve a market they've missed.

Product road maps provide insight into and clarity on decisions relating to the product line, including:

1. Development of new product and services

2. Product-line enhancements or extensions
3. Product rationalization
4. Acquisitions
5. Partnerships and strategic alliances
6. Investments in new technology
7. Operational and inventory planning
8. Resource requirements

The Product Mix

Because product managers often deal with multiple lines of product, the strategic plans they produce should reflect the ways in which the products relate to each other in the marketplace. Creating the right product mix for the company is a high-level thought process that has to account for a large number of variables.

The mix of products you sell has to meet market needs. As those needs change, product solutions change, and this means that there will be either a need for new products or a change in how useful current products are. If your product managers don't have a firm grasp on the market and its needs, it's more difficult to understand what the optimal mix of products in your product solution should be.

What's important for product managers to understand is how customer needs change. If a PM doesn't understand these aspects of his customers' businesses, then planning becomes a moot point. Those needs drive a product's life cycle, and the product life cycles drive the effectiveness of the product mix.

Getting Your Priorities Right

Whatever a product manager's plan looks like (it can be in PowerPoint as long as it isn't just a PowerPoint presentation), it must do the following: balance customer and market needs with company capabilities and business objectives.

CHAPTER 10

Monitoring Performance

If product managers have their own dilemma—responsibility without control—then so do their managers. Pushing a PM to perform in a certain way means setting up incentives to reward desired behaviors. It also means outlining in clear language what is expected of the PM. When you consider the major elements of the PM role—business owner, marketer, planner and strategist—you see that most supervisors don't effectively measure the full scope and responsibilities of a PM's job.

Focusing solely on financial metrics won't bring the desired changes in behavior that are required for a PM to truly excel in his role and ultimately produce products that dominate in the markets he serves. But therein lies the problem: how do you create succinct, definitive language to measure things like "leadership" or "influencing" while defining these things for each PM ahead of time? How do you create defined targets for each PM?

Ultimately some metrics will be compromises because you cannot put hard numbers on the soft skills we'll outline in this chapter under the category of personal performance. This will be frustrating for PMs looking for hard and fast metrics but all managers in all industries should understand that some attributes, such as leadership, are going to be judged subjectively by superiors.

For some of these traits, we'll give recommendations for how the residue of their existence can be measured. For example, a supervisor may not be able to put hard numbers on leadership but by examining the planning, adaptability, accountability and vision of each PM, he can put a picture together that confirms its presence.

Product-line metrics, on the other hand, are more straightforward and include the marketing mix, market share and sales measured against projections. These can be more specific, and they have to be because, after years of interacting with industrial manufacturers, we can say with certainty that one of the constant, major problems we encounter are the performance metrics used to monitor PM behavior. They are either missing or vague, and what most organizations just don't understand is that you get the performance and behaviors you reward. So how to begin?

First, the process of establishing PM performance metrics can begin only after the underlying support systems we've recommended are in place. That includes job descriptions for each PM and the organization-wide communication of the PM role.

Next is to divide performance metrics into strata that

reflect the experience level and expected role of each PM. For example, "intrepreneurial" PMs, whose role requires behavior that is more strategic, will need to be measured on the effectiveness of their product and market strategies. Tactical PMs, on the other hand, will be measured on their ability to effectively execute the specific components of the strategies. Because of these differing designations, the scope of evaluation has to be tailored to each PM role.

Whatever your metrics, it must be made clear to each PM what is required of him in each of the four areas of responsibility: **business owner, strategist, planner and marketer**. All four of these quadrants have to be measured and improved within the scope of two key areas: personal performance and product-line performance.

The Two Areas of Product Manager Performance

Personal performance metrics are aimed at assessing the soft skills and abilities a PM needs to perform the role and *product-line* performance metrics are designed to measure the commercial impact of the plans and strategies that are the result of the effective use of those skills.

The metrics have to be designed to determine how well the plans and strategies are working in the "real world." The assumption made with each of these metrics is that product strategies have been developed based on a thorough analysis of each market segment. If the upfront work has been done, each segment will have been analyzed to understand customer needs, including the product requirements, key buying factors that drive the purchase decisions, how customers buy (direct, distributor, retail), what type of buyers they are (value versus price, for example) and knowledge of the competitive landscape.

Assuming all this work has been done to effectively target the markets, it stands to reason that metrics should be in place to evaluate how well the PMs did in assessing the needs of the markets they serve as well as how effective they are at developing and executing the plans and strategies necessary to satisfy those needs.

We will begin with personal performance components because these are harder to define. If an organization is struggling to find people who have these soft skills, and ultimately to foster growth in these areas, then establishing performance benchmarks becomes critical.

Personal Performance Metrics

In Chapter 2, we talked about the Product Manager's Dilemma: that PMs are accountable for the success of the product line but have little or no authority over the resources that are ultimately needed to be successful.

It is within the context of this dilemma that an organization should measure a PM's ability to lead, manage and influence the expectations of the organization to achieve product-line success.

This is the art of product management: the ability to "borrow" the resources of the organization based on the ability to provide a credible argument regarding the "realities" of the business.

The following four metrics define personal performance success. For some we've included sharp measures and for others we've acknowledged that subjective measure by a supervisor is required:

9. **Leadership**: Every manager wants their PMs to lead—it's essential for their success—but how do you measure their leadership ability? Ultimately, the only way to measure leadership is by reviewing the sum total of the personal performance skills and their specific measures. Setting a "leadership" target, therefore, should be done by listing individual components of leadership that are more easily defined.

   First among these is facilitation. Forcing positive movement toward the completion of his vision for his product line, each product manager becomes a facilitator. Ultimately, success in this field comes down to one question: has the PM obtained the necessary resources he included in his plans for product-line success? If not, he may be failing in several other areas related to facilitation, including influencing, negotiation or credibility.

   If your product manager can influence his counterparts and superiors in the organization through negotiation, he can obtain what he needs. In fact, if he is credible enough, he can convince his counterparts to go above and beyond merely "helping" him and can get them to fully support his plans. Without credibility, though, influencing is impossible because negotiations fall apart.

10. **Communication**: Product managers thrive on communication, some private and some public. In order to gauge how well yours are communicating, the supervising PM in your

company can monitor several things to establish improvement goals based on performance, including presentation skills, writing and salesmanship.

Because so much of product management is about begging, borrowing and stealing what you need to get the job done, each PM has to be a bit of a showman and a salesman. Presentation skills as we define them encompass everything it takes to deliver the facts about the product manager's business and the case for the resources required to fulfill their needs. It's an odd mix of skills that includes written and oral presentations but also the ability to withstand criticism and rejection.

During the review process, you have to ask if each PM can stand up to the scrutiny that they will inevitably face when questioned about their recommendations. And can each tell the truth to the powers that be when it's not "friendly" to someone else's wants or beliefs? Do they have the courage of their convictions and, more importantly, can they sell their product ideas to an assemblage of leadership? These in-person sessions are just as important as written communications, which are also key to influencing.

One of the most frequently lacking skills among product managers is writing ability. Not everyone can write but if a PM's vision isn't well communicated in writing then a valuable form of influence is being lost. Luckily, writing classes are available to improve this skill. Monitoring this skill will mean comparing written communications against spoken explanations of a PM's plans.

Both written and spoken communications have to have an element of salesmanship in them. Each "pitch" must articulate the case for resource allocation and support, and must speak to decision-makers internally and externally. A supervisor should have each PM "sell" their product to them regularly, challenging their assertions as others in the organization will.

11. **Planning**: Planning is crucial to a PM's success. We know that without effective planning, resources can't be marshaled in time to support the product line but there's more to planning than just resource allocation. Effective planning is also adaptive planning and timely planning. The part of planning most easily defined has to do with resource management.

    Organization and time management may be the easiest personal performance skills to measure because each PM should have a game plan for how they are going to allocate their time and resources. A supervisor can review their plans and see how well they prioritize their time each week, month and year. Over time, supervisors will likely have to step in to make sure each PM isn't losing focus and dedicating too much time to tactical matters.

It's been said that "no battle plan survives contact with the enemy." The same can be true of a product or market plan. One thing is certain: once a plan is rolled out, inevitably it is going to encounter change. PMs who understand this know that they have to be adaptable and flexible enough to change as the dynamics and realities of the markets change. One measure of a good PM is how effectively they respond to the inevitability of project delays, resource limitations, parts shortages and unforeseen changes in market or economic conditions. Once their plans are completed, the real challenge of management has just begun.

12. **Management**: While product managers may not be intimately involved in every detail of life-cycle management or product development, they are required to manage the process to ensure that deadlines are met. Evaluation of project schedules and timelines can help to assess how well a PM is managing the process, meeting deadlines and moving projects forward; it is a good measure of productivity and management skill. Beyond that, though, there are soft skills to examine.

Judgment is an easily overlooked measure of PM performance because it's about reacting and thinking on the fly, which is hard to measure. Ultimately, if a PM is "getting it wrong," it may come down to judgment. Critical thinking and reasoning are at a premium in this profession and assessing how well your product managers respond to the realities of their markets means paying close attention to how well they account for the following: changing market dynamics, shifting market requirements and competitive threats. Their ability to make appropriate trade-offs will be an indicator of their judgment, critical thinking and problem-solving skills. It also reveals a rare trait: creativity.

Creativity is subjective and entirely in the purview of the supervisor, but can include areas such as new ways to segment or target markets, integrating synergistic products into solutions, inventive ways of packaging and marketing products, unique positioning strategies, even finding unique ways of securing resources; these are all measures of a product manager's creativity.

It is important that PMs have finely honed skills at not only understanding what they want and need as it relates to resources, but also what wants, needs and limitations their counterparts have that can preclude them from providing what is needed.

The criteria and measurements for success will vary depending on the role of the PM. Many times it's the soft skills of the role that are not being addressed and may not have even been considered when the initial hire was made.

The style and complexity of the metrics established will depend on the sophistication of the organization, and each of these questions will spawn specific measurements. Whatever metrics are created, they need to be indicators of how much of an impact the PM is having on the organization as it relates to product success.

Product-Line Metrics

Soft skills are necessary for a product manager to navigate the treacherous waters of matrix management. Strategic behavior, though, is ultimately what an organization wants of its PMs, and being strategic includes quantitative skills. Engineering effective metrics in these areas will not only drive growth but will drive changes in behavior.

If you truly want your product managers to be strategic, the way to do it is to focus your PMs on the one component that they truly have influence and control over: the marketing mix. That's right—the infamous 4Ps: product, place, price and promotion.

When all is said and done, the 4Ps are strategies, and PMs are ultimately responsible for developing and executing strategies that are market-focused and that drive growth. So if you want to measure PM effectiveness and change behavior, it's only reasonable to develop metrics built around each of the 4Ps. It's important that they be measured on all four because all four are essential to product-line success. Let's look at each of the 4Ps and see where metrics might be built to measure PM performance.

Product

Product proliferation and product overlaps are costly to manage and maintain. Putting metrics in place to measure the health and vitality of the product portfolio and product line goes a long way to identifying underperforming products.

At the next level there is the health of the portfolio and product mix. Assess each product to see which ones are winning and which ones are losing. Which products were contributing factors and which ones fell short of long-term goals? This helps determine which products need to stay, which need to be eliminated or de-emphasized and which future products should be embraced, and whether or not the PMs you employ are leading the charge in the right direction.

Should there actually be something lacking in the product itself, the answers the customers give as to what those problems are can inform which direction the PM needs to take in order to solve the issue. By monitoring customer relationships with the PM, an organization can better understand how in tune he is to the marketplace.

The metrics should help the PM answer questions in his mind, like: Has the product answered the needs of the marketplace and, if not, why? Has the market changed or did the product miss the mark? Is there something that has taken its place? Adding metrics will help focus the PM on the market and modify behavior to keep his or her pulse on the market. They can identify strengths or weaknesses that can be used to modify or leverage strategies. In the next generation of updates for a given product, they can be sure to include the functions the customer wants and, by doing so, can keep ahead of the market.

The metrics that reveal success in these areas are going

to be unique to each organization based on what goals and metrics it has created for its PMs. If you've done a good job of establishing goals and targets for a particular product line, then there should be metrics in place to monitor the success of those goals and targets.

At a minimum, you need sales projections in order to quantitatively measure your product's success in the marketplace, even when your organization is a service-based entity. With projections, you have a yardstick by which to measure not only the expected sales of a product but also the predictive ability of your PMs. This measurement can be broadened to include units sold, revenue per product line, gross profit, margin contribution and analysis of the product mix.

What is the competitor response? The competitor reactions are important. If the product is making headway, you should see some kind of reaction from the competition. If it's a strong effort from the competitor, then you should see them discounting or coming out with new products. If you don't see some kind of response, then you're not making the inroads that you were hoping to make. How are your competitors being impacted by your products and services?

Formal reviews of performance may be done quarterly, but the PM should be reviewing the product lines on a monthly basis. He or she can use this to project yearlong sales and then check these on a quarterly basis with staff. With these assessments, they can monitor which products are performing at a high level and which ones are not.

At the macro level, an organization should examine the entire product life cycle and management activities as a normal part of product and portfolio assessment. The central focus of life-cycle management activities is to assess the following components:

- The overall health of the portfolio
- Overall revenue and profitability
- The vitality of the product mix
- Assessment of winners and losers (top Twenty/ bottom Twenty analysis)

Life-cycle management activities provide a strategic portfolio analysis that enables directors of product management and portfolio managers the opportunity to assess the entire product line at a strategic level. This assessment is instrumental in planning for new product-development activities as well as end-of-life strategies. When PMs are armed with a strategic view of the product portfolio, product-line and product-SKU decisions can be more effectively made.

Price

Prices are generally set based on perceptions of what the market will bear. They are also set with a pre-determined expectation for gross profit or gross margin. To ensure that pricing expectations are being met, it is important to establish metrics to assess or evaluate the pricing strategy. Metrics that can be used to assess pricing could include:

- Gross-margin and gross-profit analysis
- Channel discounting (usually, there are pre-determined channel discounts, especially if using multi-tiered distribution and selling direct)
- Internal costs and the market discounts outlook

As product managers learn to monitor pricing performance, they will be able to ascertain how well the pricing strategies are doing. If there is price pressure, PMs should be able to identify it by the amount of discounting that is going on in the segments. This can be helpful in determining if the pricing model is flawed, if there is an underlying issue in the market or possibly if the product is not positioned properly. You can also adjust how you market and position the product's value in the marketplace.

Promotion

The success of market strategy, positioning and communication can and should be measured. Assessing customer acceptance of the product offering in each market should be measured.

Customer feedback includes survey data, customer service and technical support. What's more, customer concerns and reactions can lead to new opportunities because they provoke a thought process about each product and market. How is each product being used and are there new applications you haven't thought of? What are the most relevant use and market for each product? Are the physical products and services meeting the market needs? Are the products adequately positioned and priced? Are the sales channels the right ones to fulfill market-segment needs?

Place

Market-segment and sales-channel analysis is a good starting point for place. Many of our clients utilize multi-tiered sales channels, selling direct to large OEMS as well as through distributors. While product managers do not have control over the selection of the channels, they can influence which product goes where.

Product to channel analysis, or how well products sell in each channel versus expectation, is a good measuring stick for strategies and their success. This can lead to insight relative to changes or enhancements to products, product packaging and other aspects of the product offering that can impact the success of the product in the various channels.

If your PMs monitor these aspects based on pre-determined metrics and projections, they will better understand how the product line is performing. A true picture of product-line performance isn't just profit and revenue. With a good strategy in place, you should know how much growth you want and what kind of market penetration you're hoping for. With these metrics, you can perform monthly checks to see if the products are matching projections. These projections should have been generated by your PMs and vetted and approved by their managers.

Having set metrics also gives the organization the ability to weed out those employees who aren't meeting targets or don't have the vision and talent to manage the qualitative aspects of the job.

CHAPTER 11

Starting Again

So, you've done the work. You've built the systems, hired the people and set up the metrics. Now you're ready to begin.

That's right; you're now ready to begin as a functioning, high-performance culture of product management. You may be asking, "Then what was the rest of the book for if this is the beginning?"

Truly functioning as an organization with a high-performance product management organization is something that takes time and, in some cases, a good deal of change. Before judging the efficacy of these changes and effort invested, a period of "complete" operation needs to occur.

You can't judge the reliability of a car before it ever leaves the assembly line, and you won't truly have a sense of how well your product managers are working until you have the systems and the people in place. Even though you have the planning and the foundation, your people still need to execute. At this point, the life-cycle management becomes a reality.

Tactically oriented product management will still be part of what your product managers do, but we've elevated the role so that your product managers will now focus on larger, more important questions. Your product managers are now going to become market managers. They will continually assess the status of the customers and prospects in their markets and will drive the direction of your products based on their findings.

You may have some questions regarding the life cycle; most people do. Some of the questions we often get are: How do we know when a product has moved from one step in the life cycle to another? Are the lengths of the product life-cycle steps the same for all industries?

The answers are: "It depends" and "no."

It's a difficult thing to tell you that there will be specific steps to look for in the life cycles of your products. That's where your product managers come in. These steps are often dictated by myriad factors and the customer will dictate many of the steps you take based on what they perceive as important in solving the problems of the day.

Some products may have a longer life in each stage, depending on technology trends and how quickly customers are moving towards the next big problem. The reality is such because every product or industry has a different life cycle and the product managers in different industries need to be constantly assessing and analyzing the markets.

Each PM will use the systems and processes that are in place to analyze the customers' desires and how their needs and usages are changing—or not changing. This will help them understand how a life-cycle step is shifting. Then they can put the product strategies in place to answer these changing needs and stay on the cutting edge.

Regardless of their duration, there are four stages that product managers need to be aware of in the continuing life cycle:

- The innovation phase
- The growth phase
- The maturity phase
- The end of life

With the support in place, they'll be set up for a constant series of cycles that see products moving through the marketplace.

The product manager's job throughout the entire life cycle is to assess what is going on and to develop strategies as the picture becomes clearer. The organization will still sometimes fall behind the competition. But instead of reacting to gut feelings or a competitor's product or strategy, effective product managers will be in a position to build systems based on what *they* see in the marketplace. Why jump at every competitor move? You might determine that they are indeed on the right track and that gives you an edge. If so, you'll know that competing with them is the right move.

When the promise of product management is met, then product managers have everything they need to be successful. You've put a system in place to allow for broader assessment, planning and mapping. They start to drive the direction of the organization based on market needs.

The product managers can now see clearly what the market wants and now your organization knows better what it needs to do in order to become a strategically focused leader in the marketplace. They now provide information at a much higher level.

The product managers should operate through the constant quest to understand what will challenge the players in a given market and what those players will need to thrive. They should always be asking: "What's changed for the organization?"

There will be challenges in your quest to find and support product managers who are capable of managing a product life cycle. This process is not easy; it involves people, planning, systems, culture issues and continuous change in the markets. Whatever the challenges, product managers cannot be allowed to take their eyes off of the markets because it will cost you revenue, profit and market share.

If PMs have attained the skill sets we've outlined in this book, they will know the markets are shifting and when your products are going to a different stage. There will be a market to be captured during these shifts that most organizations will miss because they haven't planned for change or haven't seen it coming.

Ultimately, building a culture of high-performance product management takes a decision from the very top of an organization and then real support in the execution of that decision. This book is based on years of living inside of those decisions and what has come of the organizations who have embraced product management at is highest levels. It works—and when it does, there are drastic improvements in how organizations navigate the marketplace and dominate their space.